MUM'S
the WORD

Published by Elevate, Charleston, South Carolina.
Member of Advantage Media Group.

ELEVATE is a registered trademark and the
Elevate colophon is a trademark of Advantage Media Group, Inc.

Printed in the United States of America.

ISBN: 978-1-60194-017-9

Most Advantage Media Group titles are available at special quantity discounts for bulk purchases for sales promotions, premiums, fundraising, and educational use. Special versions or book excerpts can also be created to fit specific needs.

For more information, please write: Special Markets, Advantage Media Group, P.O. Box 272, Charleston, SC 29402 or call 1.866.775.1696.

MUM'S the WORD

A MOTHER'S LESSONS IN LEADERSHIP

STEVE GILLILAND

ELEVATE

DEDICATION

This book is dedicated to Diane, my loving wife, who brings me so much joy. Thank you for believing in me and giving me strength to believe in myself. Thank you for loving me just as I am. Thank you for your encouragement. Thank you for allowing me to experience happiness every day of my life.

TABLE OF CONTENTS

FOREWORD
by Pat Wise
(Steve's Mother)

This introduction could be seen as self-serving. The problem is I hold my son to a much higher standard than others. On September 3, 1958, at 8:23 a.m., I gave birth to Stephen Paul Gilliland, a remarkable human being. He is a disciple of our Lord who lives on the growing edge. His sharp mind is filled with insight and inspiration from his commitment to keep on reading, learning and storing up quotable quotes.

The question I am most frequently asked is, "What makes Stephen so unique?" As I am sure Stephen would tell you, I have always tried to advise him on his journey through life. One of the many things I have told him was that he would never become what he needed to be by remaining where he was. His uniqueness has always been that *he has never been afraid to risk changing.* Too many people in life get so comfortable standing; they never get moving, in any direction.

I knew from an early age that Stephen was destined to do something extraordinary. His entrepreneurial spirit and entertaining outlook make life to him a daring adventure. His first business venture was at the age of seven when he captured insects and collected a few non-living animals (road kill) to establish his neighborhood "zoo" in our basement. He charged a dime to neighborhood children and friends before they could pass through his zoo. Even when they complained that some of the animals were dead, he responded that he never promised or advertised that everything was alive. Of course, it was after this venture that Stephen would receive an early lesson in leadership from me—uncompromising integrity. I made him promptly return all of the money he had collected.

He was always pushing things to the limit. When he was nine, I put him and his older brother to bed at their assigned bed time. They had their bed time snack, watched their 9:00 p.m. program and brushed their teeth. At 9:30 it was lights out. At 9:32 I heard Stephen scream down the stairs, "Mom, can I have a glass of water?" I told him "no"—he should have gotten it before he went to bed. You see, I know my son, and it was his way of stretching his bed time into a few more minutes. He waited a minute and then asked again. This time I told him that if I heard one more "peep" out of him, I was coming up and paddling him. No more than two minutes had passed when I heard him scream, "Mom, when you come up to paddle me, could you bring me a glass of water?" I guess you might say this was an early lesson in risk taking. Of course, after I finished laughing to myself, he got another lesson regarding choices and consequences.

Regardless of how much credit he gives me for his knowledge of leadership, he has always been a person who has learned his lessons and never made excuses. When one door to happiness closed, another one opened, and he was always willing to move beyond the closed door and enter the open one. Many people in our town complained that they didn't have the same opportunities that others had. They whined about growing up in a community of steel mills and coal mines. I've always believed that there's no excuse for not blooming where we are planted. Isaiah 60:1 says, "Arise, shine; for thy light is come, and the glory of the Lord is risen upon thee." It's hard to imagine there can be any valid excuse for not rising and shining where we are today. Now you didn't think I would write this foreword without adding a little scripture. After all, Stephen refers to me as his "King James version, front row, Bible slinging, Baptist mother." And for the record—I am proud of that. Not only because it is who I am, but that he acknowledges that, and is proud of it as well. He may joke around, but I know his heart.

Speaking of heart—that is what Stephen leads with. "What comes from your heart will go to their heart," was a lesson I taught him early in life and one he now teaches others. People are more likely to follow someone who is passionate and smart than someone who is merely smart. My son is also one of the most generous people I have ever known. He has always thought of others first and his foundation is evidence of that. His work with charities such as Habitat for Humanity and Transitional Services, Inc. has made all of us very proud. His heart is as big as his ideas and this makes him all the more unique.

As you read this book, you will see his heart illuminated. You will see a person who has learned to just be him. *He has learned that sin is when one thinks they are more than they are, or less than they are, or anything other than who they are.* I am extremely proud to be Stephen's mom, and even more honored that he asked me to write this foreword. All that I have said about my son has been to lead up to this—I want to take your hand and place it in Stephen's. I want you to know each other and enjoy a friendship. This book is like a personal conversation with my son. In it he shares the most important lessons he has learned in leadership. He gives me more credit than I deserve; and as you will read, he has learned so much every day and every step of the way. Each lesson is power-packed and filled with stories, anecdotes and stunning quotes that will keep you turning pages as you read on with amazement at what Stephen Paul Gilliland has learned from the adventure of living life to the fullest.

Here is a powerful, positive book that will bring new gusto to your life. Reading it will change the way you think about leadership. And why not?

Just for the record…he may be introduced to an audience as *Steve*, but he will always be *Stephen* when he's around me. When he wasn't doing what he should have been doing, that is when I called him by his proper name, *Stephen Paul!* Enjoy Stephen's book. If you haven't figured it out yet, I am extremely proud of his accomplishments and how he treats people. He's a gem and just happens to be my baby boy.

Patricia Wise

132 Brians Court

Portersville, PA 16051

PREFACE
A Wakeup Call for Leaders

This book is a compilation of lessons on leadership and is written for a new generation of leaders—from CEOs to students considering whether they want to become leaders, and all the leaders in between who are preparing for added responsibilities. Its message is simple to state, but challenging to realize. We need leaders to run our organizations—leaders committed to stewardship of their assets and to making a difference in the lives of the people they serve.

I wrote this book to convince current and future leaders that there is a better way to lead companies—a way that builds strong, enduring organizations and benefits all of a company's stakeholders—its customers, employees and shareholders. Writing this book has been a source of great joy, affording as it did the challenge of condensing all of my leadership philosophies and my mother's lessons over 47 years into a single, logical narrative. It was only natural to use personal experiences in describing the challenges leaders face and how they can be dealt with. Throughout the book, I have endeavored to be candid, open and introspective.

We have already been told that life is about strategies, habits and rules and that leadership is about everything from "first breaking the rules" to most recently "winning." We have also been told, "Life isn't a destination, but rather a journey." Then we were told, "It's not how you start; it's more important how you finish." I personally have read some exceptional books by some exceptional authors and still keep coming back to one basic principle. Strategies, habits, rules, starts, commitments, success, winning and finishes are ALL determined by behaviors. These behaviors influence our choices, which ultimately determine our journey. Our leadership journey—our trip—requires us to make choices along the way. Regardless of who we are and where we are traveling, every day is filled with choices that ultimately determine whether we have inner peace and satisfaction at day's end. Inner peace involves making good decisions and setting the right priorities. It comes from building lasting, genuine and healthy relationships. You're only as rich as your relationships. It doesn't stem from loving things and using people, but from loving people and using things. It comes from making genuine, permanent commitments in marriage and forming lasting, unconditional relationships with your kids, your loved ones and your friends.

Unlike many books on leadership written by observers of leaders, this one is written by someone who has spent the last 25 years on the playing field, learning how to lead and working to become a better leader. My purpose is not to hold myself up as a model of virtue or success. Rather, I want to share how I dealt with the tough issues throughout my life and the lessons I learned from a Christian-principled mother. In describing the kind of leaders we need, I hope to address the difficult challenges that future leaders will face. First, I will describe how to be driven by your purpose, passion and potential. I will challenge you to find your voice, check your passion and change your outlook. Next, I will take an in-depth look at three essential dimensions of all leaders—

practicing solid values, appreciating what we have and learning to cancel all excuses and move past losses. These are either a leader's best friends or worst enemies. Finally, part three goes beyond the bottom line to look at the power of your uniqueness, what is really important and how to lead a balanced life.

My deepest hope is that these ideas will inspire a new generation of leaders. The fundamental lessons I learned from my mother are the subject of this book. They have played a critical role in enabling me to become a better father, husband, son and corporate leader. I hope they help you do the same!

Steve Gilliland
March, 2006
Winston-Salem, NC

ACKNOWLEDGMENTS

Thanks for this book must be expressed to my mother and stepfather, Pat and Dave Wise, for providing a home life that was accented with healthy attitudes and Christian principles.

Also, Diane Gilliland, my ever-loving wife, who never wobbled in her utter faith in me. She is an exceptional wife, partner, mother and best friend. Without her vision, support, guidance, affirmations and hopes, I would never have finished this book.

MUM'S THE WORD has also been deeply influenced by Sharon Alberts, a client and friend, whose level of commitment to improving the leadership in her organization has been an inspiration to me. I would also be remiss if I did not acknowledge her husband, Skip, a good friend who on many occasions has brightened my day with an email, a phone call or a box of Esther's chocolate-covered pretzels.

A high-energy thanks goes to Jane Simpson, my friend. She is so wise, ebulliently positive and brilliant.

My thanks as well to someone who was significantly supportive and who, early on, had a profound faith in this book—Dorothy Miller of Picture Perfect Speaker, a speakers bureau that markets me to the world.

And Mike Murray, thank you for all your hard work on editing and publishing *MUM'S THE WORD*.

Finally, thank you to our children—Alex, Adam, Josh and Stephen—who have made me so proud to be a parent. Their acceptance of my schedule and their love and support has enabled me to always pursue my passion of speaking and writing.

In memory of Carrie Stevenson,
my grandmother

1904-1979

L E S S O N   1

FIND YOUR VOICE

We lead by the essence of who we are as a person.

I n a sixth grade English class, my classmates and I were asked to write a poem and recite it before the class. I completed the first part of his assignment and received a challenging note from a determined, but caring, teacher, Paul Reed. "I'm impressed with your poem. Unfortunately, it is hard for me to know if these are your words. This is a fine poem. Did you copy it from somebody?" When Mr. Reed confronted me, I was shaking and cursing myself. I had not written a single word of this poem myself. When I finally admitted that I had copied it he asked, "Why?" I began spinning a story about how my older brother received most of the attention at home, and that my "real" father had left us when I was five (that part was true). I told him that being the son of divorced parents was hard and that sometimes the pressure was just too overwhelming. I also explained that I was not the only person who had copied a poem from someone else. He listened to everything I said, and then calmly made a statement that stuck with me for years. He said, "Blaming others for your problems is only a small part of what concerns me. Rationalizing that everybody else is doing it doesn't make it right either. It is important for you to learn that your life needs to be your life, and your words need to be your words. The people that you choose to let influence you will determine your life path, and the excuses you succumb to will only serve to dilute the truth and hinder your growth as a person." What he was saying was that who I am will be determined throughout the years by the people, information and circumstances that I allow to influence me. John F. Kennedy's charisma, Margaret Thatcher's fortitude, Winston Churchill's perseverance, Martin Luther King, Jr.'s eloquence and Anwar Sadat's vision of peace were seeds planted by someone else. They were not born with that voice—they acquired it.

> *The people you choose to let influence you will determine your life path, and the excuses you succumb to will only serve to dilute the truth and hinder your growth as a person.*

Your voice is what sets you apart from everyone else. It is what makes you who you are, whether it is good or bad. Remember when your parents said, "If he jumped off the bridge, would you?"

Your voice is what determines whether people will follow you. Your voice makes all the difference. It resonates with your best intentions and aspirations. It fuels your passion and allows you to rise above the mundane and make a mark. It encourages you to do great work, to be extraordinary. It energizes and unites.

It was said about one leader, "His people would follow him anywhere—but only out of morbid curiosity." Many people lead in a way that a hood ornament "leads" a car—it's out in front, but doesn't do much to steer. Leadership is the "kiss of death" for many organizations and careers. Some of the most common "myth conceptions" about leadership are:

* People are leaders because they have formal authority, titles, money or power.
* People are leaders because they're running large businesses (or their own businesses).
* People who are trained as managers can be expected to act as leaders.
* The notion that delivering currently acceptable business results is the same as practicing good leadership.

We lead by the essence of who we are as a person, so who are you? What motivates you to lead? What fears and aspirations drive you? Can you make a difference? Answer these questions and you will have a place to stand. You will also begin the remarkable journey of finding your voice. Who you are, and how you got to that point, is the essence of how successful you are as a leader and what impact you really have on other people. Your *voice* is what determines what people will learn from you and, more importantly, how far they will follow you. Your *voice* gives meaning to every journey, provides growth in every conflict, fuels purpose in every action and, when a moment of doubt occurs, resurrects a person's belief in you. Consider your roles in life. When I think of my own personal roles—son, husband, father, stepfather, brother, brother-in-law, uncle, cousin and nephew—I find myself wondering if my *voice* will impact other people.

Your voice gives meaning to every journey, provides growth in every conflict, fuels purpose in every action and, when a moment of doubt occurs, resurrects a person's belief in you.

I recently asked a group of people attending a seminar to think about who they were as a person and how they got there. I reminded them that the essence of who they are today is not something they were born with. They acquired their voice through the influence of other people. I asked them to write down the five people who have influenced them the most in their lifetime. Stop! Take out a sheet of paper and make your list. Who is it in your lifetime that has made you who you are today? Who gave you your voice? Think about your entire life to this point. I shared with them my list as I will with you.

1. Mother
2. Diane (my wife)
3. Margaret Shannon (my former secretary)
4. Paul Reed (my sixth grade teacher)
5. Mark Brooker (a former co-worker)

It took several days for me to refine my list, but I finally narrowed it down to these five people. I then took it one step further. Beside each of their names I listed what it was they gave me. Your voice is made up of several characteristics, and each of these attributes has been passed down by someone who was a part of your life. Again, I share with you my list to assist you in your quest to find your own voice.

1. Mother	Faith
2. Diane	Unconditional love
3. Margaret Shannon	Authenticity
4. Paul Reed	Compassion
5. Mark Brooker	Consistency

My mother's faith has always been a cornerstone for me. She has always said, "The trials you encounter will introduce you to your strengths." The trials she sustained and endured were great examples of faith in action. Faith is believing in that which you have not seen. The reward of faith is seeing that which you have believed. She also taught me to set my goals by my hopes, rather than my hurts. I love the story of the young man who sold papers for the Kansas City Star on the edge of town. Often he'd huddle on the windy street corners, pulling the newspapers close to him for shelter. In those days, he vowed never again to be cold and had faith that some day he would never again be cold. As a daily newspaper reader, he noticed the cartoons. He soon began drawing his own. His first, "Oswald the Rabbit," was classified as a failure. During those early days of struggle, the young man experienced personal bankruptcy, then deep emotional depression. He never lost faith and continued to draw. He later would draw Mickey Mouse and Donald Duck. His name? Walt Disney. I, too, encountered some major trials and tribulations, but with the help of a loving mother who helped give me my voice, I acquired a deeper faith that continues to grow. My job now–pass it on to aspiring leaders.

The trials you encounter will introduce

you to your strengths.

A person who exemplifies unconditional love is someone who understands your past, believes in your future and accepts you today the way you are. Who is that person? My best friend and soul mate, my wife, Diane. She has shown me that love is not something to be won or lost. It is to be offered with no conditions. Her approach to people and life is a lesson we all should learn. She also taught me to take responsibility for my failures by realizing it wasn't bad to fail. She would still love me the same. I came to realize that I would not be cherished, immortalized or revered. However, I could expect long hours and few moments of gratitude. Within our own organization, I would come to the realization that some would soar beyond my expectations and create magic inspired by my dream. They would make me glad I chose to lead. They would hear what I said, understand it, care about it and act. But whether they soared beyond my expectations or even created magic, I would be a better leader if I loved them unconditionally for their individual contributions. Thanks to Diane, I found a part of my voice that would draw people to me and not repel them.

A person who exemplifies unconditional love

is someone who understands your past,

believes in your future and accepts

you today the way you are.

Authenticity combined with passion is a leader's megaphone. The journey to greater authenticity begins when you identify the difference between what you believe and the truths you have inherited from others. Margaret Shannon, my former secretary, taught me to be more focused, centered, integrated, self-directed and purposeful. Your need for approval, acceptance, status, deference and even money diminishes as your authenticity increases. You become more dedicated to work that matters. Authenticity liberates and relaxes. It requires much less energy to maintain balance. Margaret also believed that part of your authentic self was driven by your ability to be straight-forward. I will never forget what she told me the day I was promoted. She congratulated me and said, "Tomorrow two things will be true that are not true today. First, you will be the manager of this department. Second, you have heard the truth for the last time." She warned that becoming the leader sometimes creates emotional distance, and that it was imperative for me to be my authentic self. Authenticity is being you—the person you were created to be. This is not what most literature on leadership says, nor what the experts in corporate America teach. Instead, they develop lists of leadership characteristics one is supposed to emulate. They describe the styles of leaders and suggest that you adopt them. This is the opposite of authenticity. Margaret always said that all great leaders such as Abraham Lincoln, Martin Luther King, Jr., Winston Churchill, Anwar Sadat and Margaret Thatcher shared one thing in common—they were all authentic. She then advised me to be guided by my heart, passion and compassion and be Steve Gilliland and no one else. Again, my voice was influenced and formed by a woman who had found her voice earlier in life and was willing to pass it on.

Your need for approval, acceptance, status,
deference and even money diminishes
as your authenticity increases.

At the beginning of this lesson you were introduced to Paul Reed, my sixth grade teacher. What maybe you couldn't see in this initial story was how compassionate he was. Growing up with divorced parents was not the norm in the 60's. As a matter of fact, I sometimes was angry that all of my other classmates had their mother and father living under the same roof, attending school functions together and providing an environment that I believed to be better than mine. My anger and frustration manifested itself in the form of defiance, dishonesty and lack of effort. Instead of turning his back on me, sending me to the principal's office or calling my mother, he chose to be compassionate and work with me before, during and after school. Even after I went to junior and senior high school, he would periodically check on me to see how I was doing. He never gave up on me and always displayed compassion for my situation. He would never permit me to use my situation as an excuse. However, he understood that my circumstances were unique and, at the very least, he tried to understand. He taught me that you cannot lead without compassion. It is your life experiences that open up your heart to have compassion for the most difficult challenges that people face along the journey. Far too many leaders wall themselves off from people who are experiencing the full range of life's challenges, hardships and difficulties. Unfortunately, the trends of our society shield us from the very experiences that open up our hearts. Mr. Reed taught me that every day we have opportunities to develop our hearts through getting to know the life stories of those with whom we work, taking on community service projects, having international students living in our homes, understanding the roots of discrimination and understanding that we all are not born into the same family circumstances. I learned how to develop compassion through intimate relationships with family, friends and coworkers, and through having mentoring relationships. Through the connections formed through personal sharing, people are inspired to believe in their leaders and follow them. Mr. Reed's voice was loud and clear. He made me realize that to be an effective leader, I would have to acquire a voice that included caring, sharing and compassion.

Every day we have opportunities to develop our hearts through getting to know the life stories of those with whom we work.

Leaders are defined by their values and their character. The values of a leader are shaped by personal beliefs developed through study, introspection and consultation with others—and a lifetime of experience. Working for over a decade in the same company, I witnessed first hand leaders who ranged from exceptional to wretched. Mark Brooker was exceptional! He had qualities that normally do not appear on typical leadership laundry lists. He was truly exceptional because he was always consistent. Often it takes a crisis before you realize how people will behave under pressure and what their real values are. Mark never let his values be compromised by the organization. I always respected him for being true to his values and considered him an exceptional leader. Mark taught me many things. He taught me what leadership is. He knew the difference between leadership and management. He taught me to lead people and manage things, and to lead people in such a way that they will help us manage things. He showed me how to lead from the heart—to know people are more likely to follow someone who is passionate and smart than someone who is merely smart. He helped me understand the power of commitment. He showed me the value of mutual commitment—never asking people to make bigger commitments than you are willing to make in return. He was a friend of truth and an enemy of magical thinking. He always pushed our organization to face reality and, where possible, change internal and external realities. He never made excuses. Mark not only preached good values and taught me numerous things about leadership, he followed his own advice. He never had a double standard for his employees and himself. He was always consistent in his walk. He helped me develop a piece of my voice that teaches me never to sacrifice my beliefs just to get ahead. My voice was strengthened by having an example to show me that people will respect me for being consistent and true to my values and be willing to follow me.

Often it takes a crisis before you realize how people will behave under pressure and what their real values are.

If you don't know your voice, you lack purpose. If you lack purpose, you lack direction. If you lack purpose and direction in leading, why would anyone want to follow you?

Many people want to become leaders without giving much thought to their voice or purpose. They are attracted to the power and prestige of leading an organization and the financial rewards that go along with it. But without a distinct voice, a real sense of purpose, leaders are at the mercy of their egos and are vulnerable to narcissistic impulses. There is no way you can adopt someone else's voice and still be, as Margaret taught, authentic. You can learn from someone else's voice and work with them in common purposes, but, in the end, your voice and your purpose must be your own. My mother, Diane, Margaret, Paul and Mark influenced me in ways that would leave lasting impressions—ways that were far-reaching and that would help shape me and help me to understand myself. To find my own voice, I had to first understand myself, my passions and my underlying motivations.

Without a distinct voice, a real sense of purpose, leaders are at the mercy of their egos and are vulnerable to narcissistic impulses.

Ask yourself this question. If all of your subordinates and peers at work, friends and family were attending a seminar, and they were asked to write down the five people in their lifetime who have influenced them the most, would you make their list? I often ask this question when I am speaking to leadership groups. I also make leaders do something else that I want you to take time to do.

Without looking at your wristwatch, answer the following questions. What color is the face? Does it have a second hand? Are the numbers numeric or Arabic? Does it have numbers all the way around the face or just at the 12-3-6-9 positions? What is the brand of your watch? Without looking, answer the questions. How did you do? I asked you a series of questions regarding your wristwatch to see what kind of impact it has made on you. Let's face it. It is with you every day, you look at it several times, it is there to serve a purpose and you believe you can't function without it. Yet, almost nine out of ten times when I do this exercise, people can't tell me anything about their watch. Your watch to you is what you are to other people. They see you every day, they interact with you a few times as their boss, peer, parent, sibling, spouse or friend, you serve a purpose and you believe they can't function without you. Do you impact them more than your wristwatch? If you're not on their list then I would question how much you have impacted them.

One voice can make all the difference in a person's life. One voice can be heard above the clamor of the crowd, above the noise of the street and above the stampede in the market. When a person hears that voice, they respond to it. In an instant, your voice can clarify the cloudy and simplify the complex. It can replace despair with hope and cynicism with purpose. It plainly states the unspoken, describes precisely what people feel but fear to say and calls others to action when they are paralyzed. The genius of leadership is to first find your voice so you are able to push past doubt and uncertainty. Your voice is the essence of who you are as a person. It allows you to speak the truth so others can distinguish it from spin. It establishes compelling context, while others squabble over trivial content. It influences others to take a stand before certainty arrives. It is authentically your voice, developed throughout the years, that declares the direction you will go. It unites those who would follow and divides those who will not.

One voice can make all the

difference in a person's life.

If you choose to lead, find your voice! For, without a distinct voice, you will not be able to withstand the pressure. Some will judge you unfairly, blaming you for their lack of success. Others will expect resources you cannot give, answers that you do not have and permission you cannot grant. You will be misquoted. Your judgment will be questioned. You will certainly stumble. Failure will stalk you like a predator. I thank God daily for the people in my life that helped me find my voice. The five I highlighted in this lesson are definitely my top five. However, as my journey continues, I am constantly being impacted by the people around me. Over the last decade, I have had the privilege of speaking to thousands of people all over America, Canada and Europe. These people have helped me stay focused and encouraged my voice. When I sometimes needed assurance or a renewed sense of direction, there have been many along the way that have re-energized me and filled my cup. Don't be a wristwatch for the rest of your life. Don't be seen day in and day out without making a lasting impression.

We all have the ability to make a difference in someone's life. The capacity to develop close and enduring relationships is one mark of a good leader who has found their voice. Unfortunately, many leaders believe their job is to create the strategy, organizational structure and organizational processes. They just delegate the work to be done, remaining aloof from the people doing the work. No influence. No impact. The detached style of leadership will not be successful in the twenty-first century. Today's employees demand more personal relationships with their leaders before they will give themselves fully to their jobs. They insist on having access to their leaders, knowing that it is in the openness and depth of the relationship with the leader that trust and commitment are built. Herb Kelleher (Southwest Airlines), Fred Smith (Federal Express) and Sam Walton (Wal-Mart) are great examples of leaders who found their voices then used them to make a difference and impact thousands of people. So, take a lesson from my mother and find your voice through practicing your values every day, not just espousing them. If we preach one thing and practice another, commitment is quickly lost and we lose respect. Find your voice and watch how many people follow you!

The ABCs to "Finding Your Voice"

Aspire to impact people.

Believe that you can make a difference in a person's life.

Care enough to know and know enough to care.

PASS IT ON

Respect

When you get what you want in your struggle for self
And the world makes you king for a day,
Just go to the mirror and look at yourself
And see what that man has to say.
For it isn't your parent, spouse or children
Whose judgment upon you must pass,
The fellow whose verdict counts most in your life
Is the one staring back from the glass.

You may be like Jack Horner and chisel a plum
And think you're a wonderful guy.
But the man in the glass says you're only a bum
If you can't look him straight in the eye.

He's the fellow to please—never mind all the rest,
For he's with you clear to the end.
And you've passed your most difficult test
If the man in the glass is your friend.

You may fool the world down the pathway of years,
And get pats on the back as you pass.
But your final reward will be heartache and tears
If you have cheated the man in the glass.

LESSON 2

CHANGE YOUR OUTLOOK

Change your thoughts and you change your world.

W ho do you truly admire or consider a role model in your company, community, family or circle of friends? What is it about that person that makes him or her stand out above the rest? What attributes does he or she possess that you would want to emulate? I recently spoke to an audience and asked over 100 people these same questions. Each person they named shared one common quality—a positive mental outlook.

Can something so simple actually be the secret to their success? Absolutely! Studies have shown that a positive mental outlook is very important to your success and well-being. Although it can't guarantee immediate health and wealth, it can make your life more enjoyable and rewarding—personally as well as financially. Leaders who maintain a positive mental outlook have a distinctive advantage over other people. Experts estimate that success is 80 percent attitude and 20 percent aptitude. A positive mental outlook can enrich your personal life, your relationships and your career.

Leaders who maintain a positive mental outlook have a distinctive advantage over other people.

Over the years, several studies have been conducted to determine the effect that attitude has on job performance. Martin Seligman, PhD, a professor of psychology at the University of Pennsylvania, examined positive mental outlook at a major life insurance company. In his findings, Seligman discovered that those agents who anticipated a positive response outsold their counterparts who had a negative outlook by 37 percent. Even individuals who had failed the standard industry entrance test, yet had high expectations, outsold the average insurance representative by 10 percent. I firmly believe your expectations determine your attitude and your attitude determines your behavior. Behavior, in turn, determines performance, and we all know that performance determines results. If a sports team believes they can win, then they expect to win. Those expectations can go a long way toward winning, especially when they get behind in the game.

Your expectations determine your attitude, and your attitude determines your behavior.

When a team is losing, yet believes they can win, they continue expecting to win, keeping their attitude positive even when things may be going wrong. Observe a team that believes they will win and you will see them displaying consistent behavior that keeps their level of performance at a level higher than teams that "want" to win but don't hold winning as their belief.

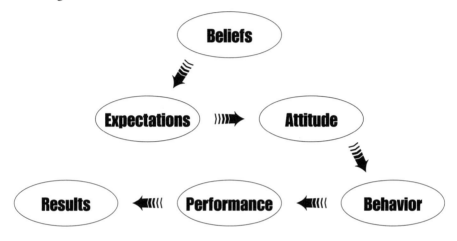

The next time you fly, take the opportunity to glance inside the cockpit at all the instruments and gauges. If you could observe a pilot in flight, you would notice they keep constant watch on one particular gauge—the "attitude indicator." I know what you are saying. "How can an airplane have an attitude?" In flying, the attitude of an airplane is the position of the aircraft in relation to the horizon. Pilots are concerned about attitude of the airplane because that indicates performance. Since the performance of the airplane depends on its attitude, it is necessary to change the attitude in order to change the performance. A leader's outlook is what I call "attitude leading" and, just like flying, your attitude indicates your performance.

Talent will determine what we do, motivation will determine how willing we are to do it, but our attitude will determine how well we do it.

Several years ago I had the pleasure of coaching midget football. The boys ranged in age from twelve to fourteen. Prior to coaching this team, I had watched them the previous two seasons. During those two years I was always amazed at the individual abilities of the players. However, their results were not indicative of their talent. In those two years they managed to win only one game. When I assembled the team for the first time under my leadership, I remember saying, "Fellows, your abilities say win but your beliefs say lose." I went on to say "Talent would determine what we did, motivation would determine how willing we were to do it, but our attitude would determine how well we did it." My job was to change the way these boys thought. They had lost for so long that they entered each game expecting to lose. Because of that expectation, the minute they got behind, it changed their attitude and caused all kinds of negative behavior. The negative behavior translated into poor performance and all the ability in the world could not change the results. To win, they would have to believe. If they believed, they would expect to win. At the beginning of every year I address the employees of our company and I keep the message clear and simple. One year I said, "If you wake up one morning and feel you are not going to have a good day, please call off sick. If you don't think it will be a good day, then I can almost guarantee you it won't be." One employee then asked me, "How many sick days do we get?" Fortunately, she was joking. However, her response made me realize that no one, not even our company, is immune to negative thinking. My job as a leader: keep my outlook positive so it sets the right example.

Our outlook is the primary force that will determine whether we succeed or fail. For some, attitude presents a difficulty in every opportunity. For others, it presents an opportunity in every difficulty. Some climb with a positive attitude, while others fall with a negative perspective. As I am writing this lesson, I am sitting pool-side in Scottsdale, Arizona, listening to several airline employees discuss the recent merger of US Airways and America West. My wife is a US Airways flight attendant. This offers me an excellent perspective of the situation. Her position is that the merger is a positive step in the right direction and she agrees with Doug Parker, CEO of America West, when he says that the two airlines are stronger together. Then there is the flight attendant who is telling anyone who will listen that the merger will never work and it's just another example of poor leadership. In one respect, she is right. Good leadership wouldn't tolerate her attitude and outlook and would replace her with someone who finds the opportunity in the merger.

> *For some, attitude presents a difficulty in every opportunity. For others, it presents an opportunity in every difficulty.*

The very fact that outlook makes some leaders while breaking others is significant enough for me to include it as an important lesson in leadership. It is an absolute fact of leadership that as a leader you will have numerous days that challenge your outlook. One of my mother's favorite sayings is, "Remember the rainbow." She always said, "In order to see the beauty of the rainbow, you have to put up with a little rain some days." It is so true. We allow people and circumstances to ruin our day. Why is it we give people permission to ruin our day? Why is it we let one person or one event in a day ruin the entire 24 hours? Life picks on everyone—don't take it personally.

The remarkable part of life is that we all have a choice when it comes to our attitude and outlook.

I shared this story in my book, *Enjoy The Ride*, but it bears repeating. On a flight from Atlanta, Georgia, to San Francisco, California, approximately 20 minutes prior to landing the pilot announced that we were about to experience some rough air and that the ride might get a little bumpy. True to his word, because of a storm, the ride became extremely rough. After we landed, the gentleman who was sitting next to me prompted me to look out the window at what he and I both described as one of the most magnificent rainbows we had ever seen. He then said, "I guess the rough ride was worth it." His point was made and again reminded me that we have to put up with a little rain some days in order to see the rainbow. Our children, relationships and professional endeavors have a sprinkling of rain and, in some cases, storms that seemingly will never end. However, our reaction to them always determines the outcome. Personally, I never thought I would survive the biggest storm of my life a few years ago, yet my mother continuously kept me focused on the rainbow. The remarkable part of life is that we all have a choice when it comes to our attitude and outlook. People blame so much of their attitude on circumstances without taking responsibility for how they react to them.

Life picks on everyone; don't take it personally.

Fumbling is part of football, failing is part of succeeding and hurting is part of loving. Every situation in life is our perception of it, not the reality of it. The glass is half empty or half full, and sometimes our perception will be based on whether we're pouring or drinking. True to form, as in most circumstances, just as the biggest storm of my life was ending, I suddenly looked up one day and saw the rainbow—the greatest gift God ever gave me, my loving wife, Diane.

As stated in previous lessons, it is important to understand what changes you can make to remember the rainbow. First, I want you to think about three things that you really enjoy doing. Next, think about three things you really don't enjoy doing. What is common to those things you enjoy doing? What is common to those things you don't enjoy doing? My guess is that you will discover that the things you enjoy doing are the ones you get to choose, while the things you really don't enjoy are the ones that leave you no choice. Dancing, reading and singing karaoke are some things you may enjoy and can choose. However, laundry, cleaning and grocery shopping are "must do's" with little or no choice. The next thing you will discover is that the "enjoy" list has rewards, while the "don't enjoy" list is non-rewarding and never-ending. What is the reward for grocery shopping? You get to put the groceries away. And which of your two lists do you control? Which of your two lists is self-assessment instead of outside assessment? If singing is on your "enjoy" list, that is total self-assessment. You choose to sing in the car and your assessment isn't critical but rather self-pleasing. On the other hand, when you consider cleaning, it is an endless task, and the assessment process is readily apparent when people visit your house. The "don't enjoy" list may cause you stress, while the "enjoy" list is relaxing. Our attitude determines our approach to life. A great example of an activity that can cause some people to relax while causing others to stress is working a crossword puzzle. If it is on your "enjoy" list, you approach it with excitement and firmly believe you will solve it. If it is on your "don't enjoy" list, your approach is different and your mindset in solving it becomes one of futility and hopelessness. Even in something this simple, our attitude determines our approach, which is precisely what happens in life.

Our attitude determines our approach to life.

Look around you. Analyze the conversations of people who lead unhappy, unfulfilled lives. You will find that they are crying out against society, which they feel is out to give them a lifetime of trouble, misery and bad luck. Sometimes the prison of discontent has been built by our own hands. The world doesn't care whether we free ourselves from the prison or not. Adopting a good, healthy attitude toward life does not affect society nearly as much as it affects us. Most days you will not get what you want. Some days you will only get what you need, but every day you will get what you expect. It would be impossible to estimate the number of jobs that have been lost, the number of promotions missed, the number of sales not made and the number of marriages ruined by poor attitudes. But almost daily we witness jobs that are held, but hated, and marriages that are tolerated, but unhappy, all because people are waiting for others, or the world, to change instead of realizing that they are responsible for their behavior. Your situations will never be all tailor-made to fit you perfectly, but your attitudes can tailor-make the situation.

Most days you will not get what you want.
Some days you will only get what you need,
but every day you will get what you expect.

Our attitude also determines our relationships with people. In leadership, your results are determined by other people. If you are a Christian, this statement should take on even more meaning since your effectiveness and ministry are based on relationships. Yet establishing fulfilling relationships is difficult. People we live beside, work with, attend church with and even live with can differ in values, vision and outlook. While you may remember the rainbow and see the best in most situations, others may see the world through a window of cynicism and regret. The key is making sure your attitude is an example of what you value and what you believe.

Nothing is as contagious as example.

Your relationship with people is determined by how closely you align with their values or how much they reflect something you love or hate about yourself. People are drawn to leaders who stand for something and have a clear view of right and wrong. Nothing is as contagious as example. People are even more attracted to leaders who display an attitude of optimism, who don't overreact to situations and who walk the message they talk. Consider the passageway created by two people who are drawn together and then discover that their values and attitudes are in alignment. If your belief is that family is the basis of a healthy life, and if your values include spending time with family, then your behaviors will include meals together, weekends and vacations together and the like. So stop reading, take a moment and ask yourself, "Would my attitude, outlook and values attract people to me or repel them from me?" Your attitude is either your best friend or your worst enemy. Your reactions to other people, however, are really just barometers of how you perceive yourself. Your reactions to others say more about you than they do about others. We are usually drawn to those who are most like us and tend

41

to dislike those who display those aspects of ourselves that we dislike. Hence, to find the rainbow in some relationships, you must practice the art of tolerance. Tolerance is when you learn to embrace all parts of others and allow them to express themselves fully as the unique human beings they are.

*Your attitude is either your
best friend or your worst enemy.*

I am completely convinced that I now enjoy leadership so much more because I stopped judging everyone else so harshly in order to feel good about myself. In my own mind, my intolerance of them rendered me superior. When you judge other people harshly, it is your way of covering up feelings of insufficiency and insecurity. I remember attending a church for several years where most of the members would sit in the same seats virtually every Sunday. I was no exception. Every Sunday I would sit in my same pew behind two ladies who always arrived earlier than most so they could fellowship (gossip) prior to worship service. When I look back on that experience, I can't help but remember some of their comments as people entered the sanctuary. "He wore that suit last Sunday. You would think he would have enough pride in himself to wear something different." "If she knew what she looked like in that dress from behind, she would never wear it again." "That skirt is way too short for church. That is an abomination…I would never…"

Before I understood leadership, I would rarely allow myself to relate to anyone who was not exactly like me. Today I find my experience more enriching because I use my judgments to learn more about myself. I have discovered that although I am different from so many people, it doesn't make them wrong nor does it make me wrong. It simply makes us who we are.

You are everything you choose to be.

When the storms of life come and you begin to run for cover, your lifelong programming will take over and the end result will be a matter of your own thought process. You are everything you choose to be. The Bible has a familiar passage which reads, "So as a man thinketh…" This biblical passage hits the nail right on the head. The human brain, that incredibly powerful personal computer each of us has, is capable of doing so much *for* us or so much *against* us. If you give your mental computer the wrong directions, it will act on those wrong directions. Those of you with children might want to pay extra attention to this particular portion of this lesson. During the first 18 years of our lives, if we grew up in average, reasonably positive homes, we were told no, or what we could *not* do, more than 148,000 times. Meanwhile, during that same period of time, how many times were you told what you *could* do or what you *could* accomplish? This negative programming that we all received, and still receive, has come to us unintentionally. It has come from our parents, who just wanted to protect us as well as from our brothers and sisters, our teachers, our schoolmates, our associates at work, our life mates and advertising of all kinds—the morning paper and the six o'clock news. As I stated earlier, your mind will give back exactly what you put into it. Behavioral researchers estimate that as much as 77 percent of everything we think is negative and counterproductive. Your brain simply believes what you tell it the most. And what you tell it about you, it will create. It has no choice.

*Your mind will give back exactly
what you put into it.*

Some people never remember, or tragically never see, the rainbows because they have been programmed not to. What if each and every day, from the time you were a small child, you had been given an extra helping of self-confidence, double the amount of determination and twice the amount of belief in an outcome? Can you imagine what tasks you might have accomplished more easily, what problems you might have overcome or what kind of leader you might be? After all, success ultimately is up to the individual. It isn't the pen; it's the writer. It isn't the road; it's the runner.

I remember being interviewed on a talk radio show as a motivational speaker and an author in the field of leadership. The interviewer's first question was, "Steve, are you one of those guys that gets people jumping in the aisles, walking on hot coals and ready to run out and conquer the world?" I know my answer surprised him. My response was, "No!" In fact, I'm very skeptical when leaders try to motivate people through an emotion. Most motivation is like a bowl of cereal—it just doesn't last long and you end up hungry in a few hours. As a speaker and author, I firmly believe my primary purpose is to get a person to realize that they are either masters or victims of their attitudes. It is a matter of personal choice. Who we are today is the result of choices made yesterday. Tomorrow will become what we choose today. To change means to choose change. As a leader, it is imperative that you evaluate your present outlook and attitude. This will take some time. If possible, you need to try to separate yourself from your attitude.

Who we are today is the result
of choices made yesterday.

First, you have to *identify problem feelings.* What attitudes can make you feel the most negative about yourself? Usually feelings can be sensed before the problem is clarified. Write them down. Next *identify problem behavior.* What behaviors cause you the most problems when dealing with others? Write them down. Third and, most importantly, *identify problem thinking.* We are the sum of our thoughts. "As a man thinks within himself, so he is." What thoughts consistently control your mind? Although this is the beginning step in correcting attitude problems, it is not as easy to identify as the first two. The next step is to *secure commitment.* "What must I do to change?" now becomes "I must change." Remember, the choice to change is the one decision that must be made, and only you can make it. Finally, you must *plan and carry out your choice.* When I can penetrate a person's heart through their mind, I have found the ultimate source of their motivation. Motivation is an inside job that is determined by the individual person. When they discover something about themselves they need to change, they make the decision, not me. By painting pictures and using real life examples, I challenge a person to take a good hard look at where they are and where they would like to end up. I also make sure that my approach is realistic and within reach but, even then, I remind myself that I provide external motivation that does not last unless the internal programming permits it.

Motivation is an inside job that is
determined by the individual person.

45

No choice will determine the success of your attitude change more than desiring to change. When all else fails, desire alone can keep you heading in the right direction. Many people have climbed over seemingly insurmountable obstacles to make themselves better people when they realized that change was possible if they really wanted it bad enough. A great example of this is the story of the frog that was trapped in a large pothole. While hopping about one day, a frog happened to slip into a very large pothole along a country road. All of his attempts at jumping out were in vain. Soon a rabbit came upon the frog and offered to help him out. He, too, failed. After various animals from the forest made three or four gallant attempts to help the poor frog out, they finally gave up. "We'll go back and get you some food," they said. "It looks like you're going to be here awhile." However, not long after they took off to get food, they heard the frog hopping along after them. They couldn't believe it! "We thought you couldn't get out," they exclaimed. "Oh I couldn't," replied the frog, "but there was a big truck coming right at me, so I had to." It is when we "have to get out of the potholes of life" that we change. As long as we have acceptable options, we will not change.

When all else fails, desire alone can keep you heading in the right direction.

If you find yourself having several bad days mixed in with your good days, stop giving people and circumstances permission to ruin your days. No one can ruin your day without your permission. Road rage is something I recognize, but have trouble comprehending. Having a total stranger pull out in front of you at a stop sign and you getting angry and giving them an obscene gesture is incomprehensible. I understand your frustration, but fail to see why you would allow that incident to have any bearing on the rest of your day, if only for a moment. Express lines at grocery stores are another great example of where you permit someone else to dictate your day. You stand frustrated, even angry, with a total stranger who ignores the "ten items or less" sign. Have you ever been in a store where they have an "express line security person" counting the items in everyone's carts? Since there are no such people, it is better to spend your time focused on something else that will allow you to remember the rainbow. I never leave home without a book or I "borrow" a magazine at the checkout counter to pass the time and keep me positively focused. You leave for the store, come home in a mood and blame someone else for it.

No one can ruin your day

without your permission.

Numerous times I have people come up to me and say, "I really enjoyed your speech and got so much out of it." My response is simple: "How will you use it?" To have people run out after hearing me speak with good intentions is exciting. To have people run out after hearing me speak with an internal action plan is life changing. I am always amazed at some players on sports teams that rely on the coach to motivate them. Great teams have individual players who are self-motivated. If it takes another person to motivate you, then you will always live your life with a multitude of peaks and valleys. The same principle is apparent when people are looking for happiness. If you are looking for a person who can make you happy, you will never find happiness.

As a leader, you also have to change your outlook regarding failure. My mother has always believed that even though failure can have a devastating effect on your life, it can also be turned into a positive experience. She has always said, "Think of failure as an education. If you don't recognize your mistakes, you will never learn from them." My mom gave me direction when I went through the most devastating time in my life. While many of my so-called friends and family were quick to judge me and jump to their own conclusions, my mother stayed true and offered the following advice.

* **Take responsibility**

    When I made the mistake, she told me to admit it immediately and tell people close to me what I planned to do to make amends.

* **Analyze the failure**

    She challenged me to figure out why I failed and learn from my mistakes.

* **Don't dwell on the failure**

    Move on! If I dwelt on the failure, it would paralyze me.

* **Keep things in perspective**

    Just because I failed at one thing did not mean my entire life was a failure.

* **Turn to loved ones**

    When you suffer a severe failure, such as I did, your true loved ones can provide you with moral support. My mother encouraged me to discuss my fears, angers and frustrations. She also reminded me that misfortune will test the true sincerity of friends and family.

* **Accept failure for what it is**

   Failure is a temporary setback. Avoid thinking of it as a life-or-death situation. Be even more determined by not focusing on people (family, friends and co-workers) who are happy you failed and who do not believe you will ever change and amount to anything. She made me realize that they have failed too.

* **Give it time**

   She constantly reminded me to give myself sufficient time to recover from the experience, but to not let it drag on too long.

* **Change your behavior**

   Prove that you learned from your mistake. Prove it to yourself only! People who are happy you failed will never see the change in your behavior…and, as mom said, "They don't need to. When they see you succeed, they will know you changed but will never admit it to you or anyone who knows you. The pendulum will swing in your favor much to their displeasure."

* **Be patient**

   Don't expect to rebuild your reputation overnight. In the meantime, concentrate on the positives.

You cannot control all circumstances. You cannot always make right decisions which bring you right results. But you can always learn from your mistakes. As a leader, failure should be our teacher, not our under-taker. Failure is delay, not defeat. It is a temporary detour, not a dead-end street. A winner is big enough to admit his or her mistakes, smart enough to profit from them and strong enough to correct them. Mistakes mark the road to success. He who makes no mistakes makes no progress. One reason some people never grow through change is that they can't stand failure. Even the best people have a lot more failure than success. The secret is that they don't let the failures upset them. They do their very best, never stop believing and let the chips fall where they may.

Failure is delay, not defeat.

In major league baseball, anyone who gets three or more hits in ten trips to the plate is destined for the hall of fame. It's a matter of percentages. In life and leadership, it's the same way. When you strike out, forget it. Strikeouts are a part of the game. If you continually believe you will win, you will expect to win no matter how many times you strike out. With the right expectations, you will have the right attitude and it will allow you to keep on swinging. Your behavior will be consistent and your performance will reap you extraordinary results.

Start exposing yourself today to successful people with a positive mental outlook. Read books that will make you a better person and a better leader. Feed your right attitudes and, before you know it, your bad ones will starve to death. Write down your successes and review them often. Share your growth with those who are interested in you and those who already have an excellent outlook. Take time daily to examine your outlook and, when applicable, thank others for making this change possible—thanks, mom! Remember—change your thoughts and you change your world.

The ABCs to "Change Your Outlook"

Accept failure for what it is.
Believe you can and you will.
Choose your attitude.

PASS IT ON

A Successful Outlook

* If you want to be distressed—look within.

* If you want to be defeated—look back.

* If you want to be distracted—look around.

* If you want to be dismayed—look ahead.

* If you want to be successful—look up.

LESSON 3

DO THE RIGHT THING

*Have an uncompromising standard
for your actions.*

How many times have I heard my mother say, "Stephen, be sure your sins will find you out?" How many times was she right? More than I care to admit in this book. At our company, Steve Gilliland, Inc., we share special beliefs about our business and the way it should be run. These beliefs—principles derived from "finding my voice," set us apart from others. We think and act differently toward our people, our resources and our business. Uncompromising standards are easy to write on paper, but difficult to maintain. They cannot be ignored. My mother and I firmly believe they are the real explanation for our success and the formula for our future.

*Uncompromising standards are easy to
write on paper, but difficult to maintain.*

The assessment of any leader starts with values, because that's where leadership starts. Values address the question, "What's important?" A leader who tells you their values and what they mean is saying, "This is what I stand for. This is what I care about." Whether one is a leader of the free world, a business executive, a department manager or a head of household, the job starts with values. These values guide us and motivate us. They connect us in a way a paycheck cannot. People are drawn to a person who has a clear view of right and wrong—a person who stands for something, a person who courageously says, "I believe in this, and I'll fight for it."

*People are drawn to a person who has
a clear view of right and wrong.*

Research shows that companies that seek to align the values of the organization with the values of the employees, and vice versa, are more fun to work for, more successful and far more focused on the needs of their employees and their customers. Companies that seek a values alignment have very few problems attracting and retaining talented people. They know what their employees want, and they know how to provide it. Values provide a common language for aligning a company's leadership and its people. A leader's role is to make the values live in the organization. They need to make them an integral part of the everyday processes of the organization: hiring, evaluating, promoting and compensating.

When you find the rare company that has established itself as truly values-driven, you can almost guarantee that it is enjoying success. Alignment around common values makes for a strong culture. The following values guide our individual actions at Steve Gilliland, Inc.

* Honor, value and respect others
* Impact people positively through encouragement, support and appreciation
* Communicate clearly, openly and honestly
* Keep all promises
* Be open to all possibilities
* Be servant hearted in attitude and actions
* Encourage professional and personal growth by continuous learning
* Be willing to take risks and learn from our mistakes
* Discover what is important to our customers
* Constantly seek to increase the quality, value and impact of our resources.

Companies that seek a values alignment have very few problems attracting and retaining talented people.

The success of building high-performance teams hinges on a leader's ability to get everyone on the same page. Once again, that process starts with clear values. Successful leaders identify and clarify their values.

When a leader has clarity concerning core values, he or she can assemble a team of people who not only have excellent skills and talents, but also "fit" with the culture the leader is creating. Importantly, a leader with a good team can go a long way toward heading off disasters before they happen. If you are lucky enough to choose your staff, like an athletic team, you are able to hire the right people. In college athletics, successful coaches not only choose the right staff that aligns with their values, but they recruit the players who also "fit" within the team's culture. Efficiency on any team is directly proportionate to a leader's ability to align his or her players around the same basic values. If you get to choose your staff, as I had the privilege of doing, you can do the same.

*Successful leaders identify
and clarify their values.*

If you inherit a team—which is typical—you need to consider some additional steps for identifying and committing to common values. First, you must have each person narrow his or her professional value choices to five or fewer. At this point, you will have a room full of teammates who have decided on their own core professional values. The goal is for these people to agree on five that the team can share. To do this, ask each person to pair with another person and decide between themselves which five are the most important. The pairings continue until you have two large groups with ten total values. The next step is to gain consensus from the group on five or fewer values. The goal is to walk out of the room with core values that answer these two questions: What do we stand for? How do we want to work together?

Clear values make for strong cultures.

When the team has identified its core values, it is time to define those values. For clarity, have your team members rate the values they've chosen. Ask them how well they are living the value as a team. For example, suppose your team picked "servant-hearted in attitude and actions" as a core value. People believe that to be a high-performing and successful team, they have to be servant-hearted in attitude and actions. On a scale of 1 (lousy) to 10 (outstanding), how well are you doing at this value? It is important to spend time defining these values so you can evaluate yourself more accurately. Clear values make for strong cultures. Leaders of strong cultures have woven the values into the fabric of their organizations so the values truly live in the daily work. Further, the leaders in strong cultures know the importance of walking the talk. There is a true and meaningful relationship between values and results. Getting everyone on the same page enhances performance. Values drive behavior.

There is a true and meaningful relationship between values and results.

In 2004, I had the pleasure of helping a Pittsburgh company seek to align its values with the values of its employees. In the end, we walked out of the room with the following core values.

* Quality of life: Encourage a quality of life as defined by the individual.

* Commitment: Be willing to take risks and learn from our mistakes.

* Empowerment: Promote a person's right to choose.

* Teamwork: Foster teamwork through clear, open and honest communication.

* Values: Be servant-hearted in attitude and actions regardless of differing values.

* Catalyst of change: Be open to all possibilities that encourage personal growth to meet individual needs.

* Basic rights: Constantly seek to protect a person's rights.

* Respect and dignity: Honor, value and respect others.

* Leadership: Lead by example.

* Balance: Never let the urgent get in the way of the important.

* Service to clients: Discover what is important to our clients.

* Integrity: Keep all promises.

Even with values, a leader will fail if he or she doesn't have the courage to say, "We just don't do that here—no matter how much money we can make." It seems so impractical. But the truth is that such a decision may be a defining moment. It can distinguish you from everyone else in your business and inspire everyone else in your organization. The only sacred cow in an organization should be its basic philosophy of doing business. Most experts agree that one of the keys to leadership is discipline.

The only sacred cow in an organization should be its basic philosophy of doing business.

In my book, *Enjoy The Ride*, I said, "When you come to the fork in the road, turn right." Numerous times I have had a person ask me, "Does it really come down to making a decision of going one way or another?" Yes! Life is about choices. Unfortunately for many, their biggest struggle is staying the course. People need to hear the same thing again and again. Staying the course is crucial. What causes so many leaders to become ineffective is that they change their course, their agenda and their goals at the drop of a hat. Discipline doesn't mean inflexibility and intractability. It does mean that the disciplined person doesn't change on a whim. In order to maintain an uncompromising standard for your actions, you sometimes have to stay the course even when it's not popular. Being disciplined doesn't mean you cling to beliefs and behaviors once you have information proving that they aren't the best ones. Being disciplined means holding fast to your basic, core beliefs but being able to adjust your actions to fit new information. If a change is necessary, the time may be as short as a day or as long as a year. Disciplined leaders stay the course and strike a balance.

In order to maintain an uncompromising standard for your actions, you sometimes have to stay the course even when it's not popular.

Doing the right thing and being disciplined involves a lot more than getting up at the same time every day, getting the proper rest and sticking to an exercise schedule. Being disciplined allows you to stay on course when you need to and helps you see when it is time to change. Being disciplined leads you to want to be responsible and accountable. It can sometimes be a thorn in your side, because you have to obey its demands. The short story is that you need to set the goals, measure the results, praise people when they succeed and hold people responsible when they fail—*do the right thing!* Being responsible means owning up to things you're less than proud of in your past behavior. I am not suggesting that a leader isn't entitled to his or her private life. However, I am suggesting that once you become a leader, you are responsible for your actions a bit more publicly. Unfortunately, that goes for past actions as well as current ones; even if past problems have no bearing on your present abilities.

Being disciplined allows you to stay on course when you need to and helps you see when it is time to change.

You stay the course because of your core values and the vision that is based on them. For the disciplined person, the difficulty isn't usually staying the course. It is in dealing gracefully with the criticism of those decisions to stay the course. Everyone else has a course, too, stressing the things that are priorities for them. If your course isn't theirs, they'll criticize. You can help them see your course by giving it to them straight—*do the right thing!* Whether you try to win them over or not, deal gracefully with criticism by agreeing in part, requesting specific feedback and using assertive communication. The key regarding a need to change is to actually know when not to stay on course. Be open and observant enough to recognize a potential need to change course. Get the information to weigh the pros and cons. What will happen if you change? What will happen if you don't change? What will happen if you don't do the right thing?

> *The key regarding a need to change is to actually know when not to stay on course.*

Another criteria necessary to *do the right thing* is holding yourself and other people accountable. The only way to deliver to people who are achieving is to not burden them with people who are not achieving. Servant leaders must be value-driven and performance-oriented. The concept of win-win suggests that leaders and employees clarify expectations and mutually commit themselves to getting desired results. Holding people accountable for results puts teeth in the win-win agreement. An effective leader is not necessarily someone who is loved or admired. He or she is someone whose followers do the right things. Popularity is not leadership. Results are. Leaders who do the right thing and get the results earn something more beneficial than praise. They earn respect. My mom has always said, "I would rather have you respect me for my beliefs than like me for letting you get away with something."

> *Popularity is not leadership.*

Good leaders make it easy for their team to get results. They pave the way for success using tools of decisiveness and clarity. If there is a single complaint that resonates loudest from disgruntled workers, it is that their leaders can't make up their minds or that they make a decision and then change it the next day. Decisions should be made thoroughly, thoughtfully and fairly. After making a decision, it is important to act decisively as well. Decisive action is good because it provides clarity for workers and a sense of urgency. Good leaders light a fire in the belly of their troops. The key is not to second guess you. Make a decision as soon as it comes across your desk and then move on to the next one. When you make a mistake, don't dwell on it. Rather, learn from it. In order to hold people accountable, it is imperative to be decisive and provide a level of leadership from which it is easy to get results.

Decisions should be made thoroughly, thoughtfully and fairly.

It is extremely important to bring in the right people. Teams need to feel that everyone is capable of pulling their own weight. When this is not the case—when one person continually fails to produce or measure up—a leader must act or team morale will suffer. To boost morale, it is necessary to express sincere appreciation of workers' hard work and dedication. You must value them and tell them so. Recognizing employee excellence in meeting the targets set by the team is also very important. Your goal must be to make your staff feel good about working for you. All the research shows that motivated employees are generally more productive employees, and productivity equals results. The key is to make sure you are genuinely interested in people. People will never care about the results until they know you care about them.

Teams need to feel that everyone is capable of pulling their own weight.

Should accountability and results be considered in this lesson entitled *"Do the Right Thing"*? Do leaders really have to hold their people accountable and pave the way for excellent results? Yes, according to the research done by Bruce N. Pfau at Watson Wyatt Worldwide (www. watsonwyatt.com/research/). In fact, Pfau's study provides evidence that holding employees accountable for performance—rewarding them for outstanding results and terminating chronic non-performers—is not only the right thing to do, it is the largest single contributor to a company's stock performance, even ahead of hiring excellent people. The HCI study showed an average of a 16.5 percent increase in the stock price of companies with leaders who reward employees for good work, refuse to accept sub par performance, offer excellent pay and benefits, link pay to company performance, promote competent employees, help poor performers and terminate chronic non-performers. How do you get accountability and results? Do the right thing—read and heed.

* Have a clearly articulated strategic direction that will enable you to succeed against competitors.

* Help followers focus on a few key priorities and clearly stated goals.

* Recognize and reward success and take action on employee problems.

* Gain widespread agreement on necessary roles and accountabilities.

* Hold people accountable to the highest standards of performance.

* Create a sense of urgency and drive to succeed.

* Make decisions on tough issues in a timely manner.

* Give people the resources and autonomy they need to be successful.

* Invest in and support the development and education of employees.

In an era when almost every corporation rightly has a statement of values (even Enron had core values), it is necessary to reflect on how well you are upholding your personal and professional values. You must flexibly adapt to new conditions while finding ways to remain true to your fundamental beliefs. My mother's lesson in always doing the right thing has helped me on my journey to learn new cultures and new markets, adapt to new technologies and face many other challenges. Individually, what you stand for gives you clear guidance on your priorities and work practices. Blended together, they help you behave correctly in the most complex situations. Because if you don't—"Be sure your choices will find you out."

The ABCs to "Do the Right Thing"

Assess your values.

Be open and observant enough to recognize a potential need to change course.

Constantly hold fast to your basic, core beliefs.

PASS IT ON

Take Time to...

* **Think**—it's the source of power

* **Play**—it's the secret of youth

* **Read**—it's the foundation of wisdom

* **Be friendly**—it's the road to happiness

* **Laugh**—it's the music to the soul

* **Give**—it's the price of success

* **Love**—it's the greatest power on earth

LESSON 4

STAY OUT OF THE RUTS

Change is a journey waiting to be taken.

Everyone gets in a rut. Even motivational speakers who write books and make their living trying to inspire and motivate others get in a rut. Every leader has moments of doubt and insecurity. They come upon an obstacle they believe to be insurmountable or find a frustrating, seemingly intractable barrier interrupting the path to success. Try as you might, you will never find a person whose life was exactly the way that person wanted it to be from the day he or she was born until death. No matter how rich, powerful, intelligent, beautiful, famous, successful or admired you are, you can take a wrong turn, lose your way, skid off the road and find yourself knee deep in quicksand and sinking fast. At least once in a lifetime, and more likely many times, you and I get in a rut and get stuck.

Every leader has moments
of doubt and insecurity.

The good news is everyone who gets in a rut can get out. Bad marriages, dead-end jobs or even feeling alone and isolated in a new town are some of the most obvious painful places to be stuck. When we get ourselves into these frustrating and self-destructive situations, only one element is common—change is required. The problem is we can't seem to make change happen. Nothing seems able to get you moving—not your desire to do better, not your treasured goals and aspirations, not even the pain you feel. Threats, bribes and impassionate pleas are not enough to move you.

When we get ourselves into frustrating and self-
destructive situations only one element
is common——change is required.

Joan, a forty-five year old registered nurse from California, lamented to me about being in a rut the last time I spoke at a meeting her hospital sponsored. She said, "Now that I am a supervisor, I don't work with people anymore. I work with paper. Forms, files, memos and medical reports are the main scope of my responsibilities. It almost seems that no one cares what you do with the patients as long as the paperwork gets done on time. I took this job because I wanted to serve people, but I ended up serving the system. If you started out caring, the system or a person who works for you beats it out of you." Like most people who find themselves trapped in an intolerable situation, Joan did not get to the end of her rope overnight. She had slowly painted herself into a corner by the choices she made, the real injustices and indignities of her job and all she had not done to turn things around earlier in her career and her life. Numerous people find themselves in the same scenario as Joan. Ever been in a bad relationship? Even though you know that leaving the relationship is what you should do, you rationalize why you are better off staying. You begin to yell at the children more, stay in bed longer and tolerate a living hell. Worse yet, you begin to believe your own propaganda and say, "What can I do? I made my bed, now I have to sleep in it. How can I risk losing what little I have? There's nowhere to go. I'll get by somehow."

People who find themselves trapped

in intolerable situations did not get to

the end of their rope overnight.

Sound familiar? Those are all sounds of resignation, of settling for the way things are, of putting up with jobs, relationships and circumstances that are less than you desire—or deserve. You know you are in a rut when these six things are true.

* You see few or no alternatives to your current situation.

* You allow fear of failure, disappointment, rejection, loss or change to keep you from taking risks.

* You become fatigued and depressed in many areas of your life.

* You begin to complain more often than you used to, seeing only the dark side, taking every opportunity to point out how bad things are, believing all available options are doomed to fail and rejecting them outright.

* You grasp at straws or go to extremes, without careful consideration or planning, pursuing the first alternative that presents itself.

* You start projects, diets, exercise programs or any other self-improvement effort and abandon it soon after you begin, halfway through or one step before you reach your goal.

Being in a rut is finding yourself back at square one and wondering if you have the strength to start over. When I look back at the times I got in a rut during my leadership career in corporate America, I, too, wondered if I had the strength to start over. In the speaking business, people get in ruts that sometimes cost them a career. They want to make a change and don't know how. They begin to listen to other speakers, pursue alternatives too fast and end up in a bigger rut than they were in. The changes they need to make elude them, and the changes they do make doom them. They spin their tires without moving forward and soon they are in deeper than before. How many times has a person dieted, lost ten pounds, got back in a rut and put on twenty pounds? How many times has a person refinanced their mortgage, took out a second mortgage, paid off their credit cards and ended up deeper in debt? Frustrated, we push the gas pedal harder, eat more and become apathetic to the credit card bills that will soon arrive. But what can you do?

People stay in a rut because the changes
they need to make elude them, and the
changes they do make doom them.

In my book, *Enjoy The Ride,* I said, "The true joy of life is in the trip." Neither the beginning of the trip nor the end is as important as the journey itself. If life is a journey, then being in a rut is a detour. The road of life twists and turns, sometimes by choice, and sometimes because unforeseen obstacles impede your progress. Occasionally you lose your way altogether. Everyone does! I have seen leaders get all packed and ready to go but never make the trip. Some leaders set out with the greatest of intentions but turn back at the first sign of stormy weather or get halfway to their destination and panic. Fear brings you to a standstill and you wonder if you truly want to continue the journey. You don't know exactly what lies ahead of you and worry that getting to where you are going might not make you happier. So you turn back or stay where you are. No matter which detour you take, you arrive at the same outcome. You find yourself somewhere you did not plan to be or want to be—and you do not know how to get out of the rut. Everyone gets in a rut because certain roadblocks cause them to reroute, postpone or abandon their journey. As a leader, you have the tools to tear down the roadblocks, but you can only change if you choose to do so. Change is a journey waiting to be taken.

Everyone gets in a rut because certain
roadblocks cause them to reroute,
postpone or abandon their journey.

One of the first roadblocks is low self-esteem. Negative criticism, perceived failures and trying to measure up to other people's standards damage your self-worth and lead you to believe you do not deserve better or more than you have. Growing up in western Pennsylvania in the 60's offered a roadblock to me and other kids. We were indoctrinated with a belief that unless we were a child of the affluent families of our area, the steel mills were as good as it would get. Hundreds of graduates from local high schools never even applied to college believing they were not worthy and had everything that life offered someone growing up in western Pennsylvania. Thank God for a mother who believed that I could be anything I wanted if I was willing to pay the price. Her version of *The Little Engine That Could* was a bit different than most. She would read it, "I know you can, I know you can, I know you can." Believing you do not deserve better is the bottom-line roadblock to change. More debilitating than the pain and confusion of your present circumstances might be, it stands in the way of your sincere desire to change. It prevents you from clearing other obstacles in your path. No matter what you say you want, you will not leave the rut unless you believe you deserve a better life and are capable of change. Parents, teachers and ex-spouses are the first critics who implied you would never measure up. Today the voice is your own. You have come to believe you are unworthy, unlovable and deserving of the fate life deals you—and nothing more.

Believing you do not deserve better is the bottom-line roadblock to change.

There is no easy formula to overcome this roadblock, but I can offer two things that will help. Think of three people who you believe have high self-esteem, people who like themselves and have a positive opinion of their own worth. Think carefully about the qualities these people possess. As I have stated before, the key is to surround yourself with a character of people that resembles who you want to be. You must be cognizant of who they are and what makes you believe they have a good self-image. These mentors can pave the way by showing you how to believe you deserve better and go after what you want. Early in my career, I was blessed to work around a woman who I perceived to have high self-esteem. She had a great sense of humor, was friendly and was able to say "no" to people. I carefully watched how she handled situations and even sought her advice. Then Margaret came into my life and offered me the second thing that will help you believe you deserve better. She taught me how to take more risks. She challenged me to take intellectual risks by reading more books, attending more seminars and engaging in more stimulating conversations. She helped me see the world from other points of view. She helped me expand my horizons by gaining appreciation, skill and understanding of art, music, theatre and computers. She challenged me to know more than I knew. I would also offer this advice to some of you reading this book. Take emotional risks. Go new places. Meet new people. Start conversations. Return a smile. Join a singles group. Accept a blind date. Ask for a raise. Express your ideas. Assert yourself. Disagree. Be the first one to say, "I love you." There is no easy formula for breaking down this first roadblock, but once you do, your emergence from the rut is eminent.

Surround yourself with a character of people that resembles who you want to be.

The second roadblock that keeps you deep in a rut is not seeing alternatives. In leadership, without options you have no place to go. Without the decision-making skills to choose options and without the ability to follow through with a plan, you spin your wheels and go nowhere. Without realizing you have alternatives, you have no vision to guide you when a choice must be made. Without all your options, you have no destination to move toward and no reason to alter your course. You stay where you are because you simply cannot determine any new direction.

> *Without realizing you have alternatives,*
>
> *you have no vision to guide you*
>
> *when a choice must be made.*

A former colleague of mine remains in a rut because of this roadblock. When I met Joe in 1999, he was facilitating seminars for a large seminar company. Just like me, he was accepting contract work to speak for this company that arranged the seminars, the travel and basically controlled the schedule. Joe was an exceptional speaker and had outgrown this seminar company. I remember discussing with Joe the vision I had to become independent of this company and arrange my own speaking engagements. The irony—Joe had been doing contract work with this company for over ten years and I was in my first year. Underpaid and overworked was the mantra for an exceptional speaker who would stay on this maddening circuit more than a couple of years. When I told Joe about my vision, I remember him rejecting my alternatives one by one. His comeback for every suggestion was, "Yeah, but…!" I was convinced that no matter what alternatives I offered him, he would always be able to find legitimate reasons why the alternative plan of action might not work.

When you are in a rut, you may not notice that the probable positive outcomes of changing your situation far outweigh the possible negative consequences. When you are in a rut, the flaws are all you see. As a result, you may pass up reasonable avenues for getting unstuck because smooth sailing and a direct, uninterrupted road to complete happiness cannot be guaranteed. Today, Joe is still contracting all of his speaking engagements through the same seminar company and will probably leave this earth never realizing that if he would have pursued the alternatives he would be working less, spending more time with his family and making a whole lot more money.

When you are in a rut, you may not notice that the probable positive outcomes of changing your situation far outweigh the possible negative consequences.

Just as in Joe's scenario, alternatives do exist. You get in a rut when you don't know how to recognize them. You feel trapped because you have not found viable options—yet. But you can learn how to look for them. When you do, you will find them. Of all the barriers to change, this one is the easiest to dismantle. Why? Alternatives do exist. There is always at least one option and usually many more. There is always something you can do or stop doing. Merely realizing alternatives do exist relieves stress and counteracts that desperate feeling you get whenever you believe you are trapped in a corner with nowhere to go. The alternatives you find may not be perfect. They may not show results immediately or completely or magically alter your existence. Alternatives are not all you need to get out of the rut or achieve your goals. However, learning to recognize all your options is a step. A step is movement, movement that can bring you closer to your chosen destination. So, Joe, if you read this book, realize that I exercised my options, and, although some were not perfect and the results were slower than expected, I am now enjoying my family more, traveling less and earning more money in a month than I used to earn in a year.

There is always something
you can do or stop doing.

Roadblock number three is supported by the first chapter of my book, *Enjoy The Ride*. Confused by conflicting messages about what you should do and be, you let parents, preachers, advertisers or the "Joneses" set priorities for you. The roadblock: Not knowing what you really want. Without a clear sense of what you value, you lack the vision to accomplish your goals. My stepson, Adam, and I have had our moments and, at times, I have felt like he was in a rut—and yet I am public enemy number one when it comes to confusing him about what he should do and be. When I ask Adam what he really wants, I basically am asking him what he really values. Values are guides for daily living that influence your thoughts, feelings, words and deeds. They shape your personality and give you direction to what would otherwise be an aimless, purposeless life. Your values are reflected in your goals, hopes, dreams, attitudes, interests, opinions, convictions and behavior, as well as in your problems and worries. Everyone has values—even my sixteen-year-old stepson, Adam. Some people simply understand their values more clearly than others. They realize values affect all aspects of their lives. Seeing the connection between values and actions, they act consistently with commitment.

When Adam begins to know and live by his values, he will take steps to consciously develop and clarify those values. For now, my job is to support him and influence him in a positive way and not confuse him about what he should do and be. You can take the same steps and they will pay off in the same way. Regardless of whether you are 16 or 60, you will end up knowing what you really want, and you will improve your chances of getting it. I do not guarantee that clarifying your values will get you everything you want or remove every obstacle from the road you travel. However, from personal experience and years of observation, I can honestly say that value clarification will help you make self-enhancing rather than self-defeating decisions, gain realistic perspective on your life and shape a vision of the way your life can be in the future. For Adam, only time will tell, as he sorts out his values and begins to figure out what he really wants.

Your values are reflected in your goals,

hopes, dreams, attitudes, interests,

opinions, convictions and behavior,

as well as in your problems and worries.

Another major roadblock is fear. The prospect of changing frightens you. Change brings with it the possibility of failure, rejection, disappointment and pain as well as the chance that getting what you think you want will not solve your problems after all. Fear causes you to sacrifice probable gain so you can avoid possible pain. Fear is a powerful and quick teacher. Its lessons are learned at the gut level—and are rarely forgotten. There are no slow learners where fear is the teacher. Think of the young child who learns not to touch a hot stove. The very first time he touches the stove, he gets the message, and he does not have to think long and hard about it. He gets burned and immediately decides that he does not want to feel pain like that again. So he stops touching hot stoves. Throughout your lifetime, you learn similar lessons in the same way. You learn to fear and avoid much more than physical pain, however. You have been hurt before. You have been disappointed, rejected, embarrassed or belittled. You have lost things you cherished and failed to get what you wanted. When you remember these experiences, they stimulate all sorts of painful, negative emotions. The thought of feeling these emotions again frightens you, and you begin to avoid any situation or circumstance that presents the possibility of disappointment, rejection or embarrassment. As a result, your fears and avoidance behaviors limit the number and kind of risks you are willing to take. Here are ten ways fear blocks change.

* Fear persuades you to set easier goals and do less than you are capable of doing,

* Fear triggers your internal defense system and fools you into thinking you have perfectly good reasons not to change.

* Fear reduces the number of available alternatives or keeps you from pursuing them.

* Fear causes indecisiveness and confusion. It stops you from knowing what you really want.

* Fear warps your perception of life and what you can do to make it better.

* Fear keeps you from asking for help when you need it or benefiting from the emotional support offered to you.

* Fear keeps you from asserting yourself and persuades you to settle for what you feel you must settle for instead of going after what you want.

* Fear causes you to develop unhealthy habits and behavior patterns.

* Fear often makes you give up just one step short of your goal.

* Fear keeps you from taking risks.

To rid yourself of fear and regain lost control, you must lure the monster out of his cave and whack him on the head until he can no longer harm you. (OK, so I am writing this lesson as I fly from Charlotte to San Francisco and have had a couple of cocktails). Without cocktails, the translation would be you have to face your fears by acknowledging them and then confronting them. You must take a good long look at your fears and see how they limit you. Then you will be able to take steps to counteract those fears, control your anxiety and move forward once again.

Fear causes you to sacrifice probable gain so you can avoid possible pain.

And what would this lesson be without disclosing yet another one of my many flaws—perfectionism. You want a guarantee. You want a perfect solution and a perfect unobstructed road to your goal which must yield perfect results. For you, or at least for me, it's perfection or nothing. With that ultimatum, you can never achieve what you want. When I diet, I expect nothing less than perfect adherence to my food plan. The trouble for me is that "right" means perfect. The curse of perfectionism undermines change so brilliantly because this roadblock never works alone. It teams up with other roadblocks to more efficiently get you in a rut and keep you there. This roadblock invites the return of the first roadblock—believing you don't deserve better. As I looked for the perfect spouse, I could not find her. I believed that because of my past failures I was not good enough so, therefore, I did not deserve happiness. Self-esteem takes a nose dive and stops you cold. The sad thing was that because of my obsessive attitude towards perfectionism, I was doomed before I even began. My solution was to become excellent instead of perfect. Perfectionism is defined as *"complete and flawless in all respects."* Excellence is defined as *"outstanding, good or of exceptional merit."* I knew I could achieve excellence and that was a more realistic expectation and a worthy goal. My wife, Diane, knows that I do make mistakes. However, I am exceptional at many things. In addition, aiming for excellence allows forgiveness. When you seek excellence, you accept the fact there are no absolutes. There will be bad days and you will make mistakes. There will be setbacks and temptations you should, but do not, resist. The perfectionist focuses on the flaw and not the whole. The seeker of excellence looks at the big picture, recalls the good already done, forgives the error and gets back on track.

*The perfectionist focuses on the flaw
and not the whole.*

Perfectionism negates the value of progress while aiming for excellence rewards progress. To achieve your personal best, you simply try to do a little better each day. You may be a long way from your destination, but each time you master a step and achieve excellence at that level, you have cause for celebration. You have progressed and progress is excellent.

The ABCs to "Staying Out of the Ruts"

Acknowledge you are stuck.

Begin to understand why you resist change and create a plan to change.

Change the way you see yourself.

PASS IT ON

I'm Glad You're in My Dash

I read of a man who stopped to speak
at a funeral of a friend.
He referred to the dates on her tombstone,
from the beginning to the end.

He noted that first came her date of birth
and spoke the following date with tears,
but what mattered most of all was the
dash between those years. (1934–1998)

For the dash represents all the time
that she spent alive on earth,
and now only those who loved her
know what that little line is worth.

For it matters not how much we own —
the cars, the house, the cash,
what matters is how we live and love
and how we spend our dash.

So think about this long and hard —
are there things you'd like to change?
For you never know how much time is left,
that can still be rearranged.

If we could just slow down enough
to consider what's true and real,
and always try to understand
the way other people feel

And be less quick to anger
and show appreciation more
and love the people in our lives
like we've never loved before.

If we treat each other with respect,
and more often wear a smile,
remembering that this special dash
might only last a while.

So when your eulogy is read
with your life's actions to rehash,
would you be proud of the things they say
about how you spent your dash?

LESSON 5

ACCEPT LIFE ON LIFE'S TERMS
Lessons learned—wisdom earned.

Y
ou can only teach people so much. You must be willing to let people make mistakes or they'll never achieve their potential. One of the most desirable attitudes of a leader is their ability to view problems as opportunities and setbacks as temporary inconveniences. This positive attitude also welcomes change as friendly and is not upset by surprises, even negative surprises. How we approach challenges and problems is a crucial aspect of our decision-making process and will ultimately determine our ability to learn the lessons from our mistakes. All lasting success in life is laced with problems and misfortunes which require creativity and a whole new way of juggling personal and professional priorities. When I was growing up, my mother always had our family organized around my brother and me, and everything was about our faith, education and opportunities. My mother always told me to follow what I was passionate about and to believe that the only obsta-

cles you're going to have are the ones you fabricate for yourself. I always felt supported and accepted. No mistake was so big that you couldn't go home and talk about it.

All lasting success in life is laced with problems and misfortunes which require creativity and a whole new way of juggling personal and professional priorities.

Nothing in life breeds resilience like adversity and failure. A study in *Time* magazine in the mid-1980's described the incredible resilience of a group of people who had lost their jobs three times because of plant closings. Psychologists expected them to be discouraged, but they were surprisingly optimistic. Their adversity had actually created an advantage. Because they had already lost a job and found a new one at least twice, they were better able to handle adversity than people who had worked for only one company and found themselves unemployed. I truly believe that if you are interested in success, you have to learn to view failure as a healthy, inevitable part of the process of getting to the top. The benefits of adversity often outweigh the pain of failing. Life has an interesting way of testing all of us to see if we can embrace adversity and persevere through it. Maybe the toughest lesson in accepting life's terms is learning that with most problems there is a need to change.

If you are interested in success, you have to learn to view failure as a healthy, inevitable part of the process of getting to the top.

In 1997 I went through the most difficult time in my life. I will always remember my attorney saying to me during a lunch meeting, "You can't see it now, but some day you will look back and realize that everything you are going through right now will determine your future depending on how well you handle it." He said, "People will expect you to stay down, give up and lose all motivation to ever succeed again. Your ability to accept change and stay positive through it will be the key to your future." I also remember being heart sick that people who I thought were my friends turned their backs on me and went on with their lives like mine never mattered. It was like some people were happy that I had failed and had hit the bottom. My inner circle of people had diminished to two—my mother and my best friend. My best friend, Todd, would continually preach to me the same sermon every time we were together. He said, "Adversity can make you better if you don't let it make you bitter." How true that is! Why? It promotes wisdom and maturity. Ten years later I have turned the most difficult time in my life into a testimonial of what happens when you accept life on life's terms and grow wiser and more mature.

> *Adversity can make you better*
> *if you don't let it make you bitter.*

American playwright, William Saroyn, spoke to this issue. He said, "Good people are good because they've come to wisdom through failure. We get very little wisdom from success, you know." As the world continues to change at a faster and faster rate, maturity with flexibility becomes increasingly important. These qualities come from weathering difficulties. Harvard business school professor, John Kotter, says, "I can imagine a group of executives twenty years ago discussing a candidate for a top job who had had a big failure when he was 39. Everyone would have said that was a bad sign. I can imagine that same group considering a candidate today and being worried because the candidate had never failed or faced adversity." The problems we face and overcome prepare our hearts for future difficulties. I recently had the pleasure of sharing the platform with Robert Danzig, CEO of Hearst Newspapers, who authored the book, *The Leader Within You*. His opening statement was, "People ask me all the time how to become the CEO of a billion dollar company? It is simple. You get fired from your first full time job." When you eliminate problems from the equation, it limits your potential. Virtually every successful entrepreneur I have met, or read about, has numerous stories of setbacks that opened the door to greater opportunity.

The problems we face and overcome prepare our hearts for future difficulties.

One of my mother's favorite statements has always been, "Stephen always pushes the envelope." I do. Guilty as charged. But I personally believe that until a person learns from experience that he can live through adversity, he is reluctant to buck mindless tradition, push the envelope of organizational performance or challenge himself to press his physical limits. Adversity prompts a person to rethink status quo. When circus performers learn to work on the trapeze, they know that the net below will catch them, thus they stop worrying about falling. You can actually learn to fall successfully. What this means is you can concentrate on catching the trapeze swinging toward you, and not on falling, because repeated falls in the past have convinced you that the net is strong and reliable when you do fall. Falling and being caught by the net results in a mysterious confidence and daring on the trapeze. You fall less because each fall enables you to risk more. In leadership, adversity pushes the envelope of accepted performance. If you are fearful of adversity, you will always make decisions based on a "risk free" mindset that sometimes will cause you to miss incredible opportunities for growth.

Until a person learns from experience that he can live through adversity, he is reluctant to buck mindless tradition, push the envelope of organizational performance or challenge himself to press his physical limits.

When Mary Kay Ash (Mary Kay Cosmetics) visited her attorney to make legal arrangements for her new corporation, he insulted her and predicted her failure. "Mary Kay," he said, "if you are going to throw away your life savings, why don't you just go directly to the trash can? It will be much easier than what you are proposing." Her accountant spoke to her in similar terms. Despite their attempts to discourage her, she moved ahead. She sank her $5,000 life savings into her new business—every cent she had. She put her husband in charge of the administrative side of things as she worked feverishly to prepare the products, design the packaging, write the training materials and recruit consultants. They were making wonderful progress. But a month before she was to open her business, her husband died of a heart attack right at their kitchen table. Most people would never have been able to go on after that. They would have accepted defeat and faded away. Mary Kay did not. She kept going, and on September 13, 1963, she launched her business. Today, the company has more than 1 billion dollars in annual sales, employs 3,500 people and empowers 500,000 direct sales consultants in 29 markets worldwide.

Mary Kay Ash has received just about every award an entrepreneur could dream of. Despite adverse circumstances, obstacles and hardships, she accepted life on life's terms and succeeded beyond expectations.

> *Many people miss opportunities*
> *because they focus on what is missing*
> *rather than on what they have.*

The average person makes a mistake and automatically thinks it's a failure. But some of the greatest stories of success can be found in the unexpected benefits of mistakes. For example, most people are familiar with the story of Edison and the phonograph. He discovered it while trying to invent something entirely different. But did you know that Kellogg's corn flakes resulted when boiled wheat was left in a baking pan overnight? Or that Ivory soap floats because a batch was left in the mixer too long and had a large volume of air whipped into it? Or that Scott towels were created when a toilet paper machine put too many layers of tissue together? Horace Walpole said that, in science, mistakes always precede the truth. I believe that in leadership, mistakes always precede great leaders. The hard lessons you learn along the journey are always more valuable than the textbook definitions of how you should handle any situation. One of my favorite expressions is, "Been there, done that, got the hat, T-shirt, keychain and a bumper sticker." As a speaker, I get concerned when I hear a speaker discussing customer service and I know for a fact they do not return phone calls. I am equally as concerned when I hear someone presenting a program on leadership and know for a fact they have never held a leadership position. My concern is that unless you have experienced what you are talking about, chances are you never experienced the adversity that accompanies that experience. I am not suggesting that to be a great leader you have to face adversity and challenges. However, I am suggesting that if you are in leadership, you will face adversity and challenges and your greatness will not be in facing them, but in how you handle them.

> *The hard lessons you learn along the journey are always more valuable than the textbook definitions of how you should handle any situation.*

I also discovered that adversity and challenges motivate great leaders. The manner in which a person faces adversity tells so much about that person. Does adversity motivate you, or does it make you overreact, sulk or, in many cases, quit? Years ago when my son, Josh, was playing in a high school football game, his team was ahead by only six points in a game with less than two minutes remaining in the fourth quarter. The coach sent Josh, who was the quarterback, into the game with instructions to play it safe and run out the clock. In the huddle, Josh said, "Coach said play it safe, but that's what they're expecting. Let's give them a surprise." With that, he called a pass play. When Josh dropped back and threw the pass, the defending cornerback, who was an all-conference sprinter on the track team, intercepted the ball and headed toward the end zone, expecting to score a touchdown. Josh, who was a decent runner, but not a sprinter on the track team, took off after the cornerback and ran him down from behind, tackling him on the 5-yard line. His effort saved the game. After the clock ran out, the opposing coach approached my son's coach and said, "What's this business about your quarterback not being known for his speed? He ran down my speedster from behind!"

Josh's coach responded, "Your man was running for six points. Josh was running for his life." Nothing can motivate a person like adversity.

> *The manner in which a person faces adversity tells so much about that person.*

One of the best stories I've ever heard of someone who learned to accept life on life's terms and who refused to take failure personally is that of Daniel "Rudy" Ruettiger, a kid who desperately wanted to play football for Notre Dame. You may have seen the film based on his life called *Rudy*. It was a good movie—one of my favorites—but his real story is even more remarkable and compelling. The first of fourteen children in a poor working-class family, Rudy loved sports as a kid and believed sports might be his ticket out of Joliet, Illinois. In high school, he gave himself completely to football, but his heart was much greater than his physique. He was slow, and at five feet six inches and 190 pounds, he wasn't exactly built for the game.

As a senior, he began dreaming about attending Notre Dame and playing football there. But Rudy faced another problem. His grades showed less promise than his physique. "I finished third in my class," he was fond of saying, "not from the top, but from the bottom." He was a D student. He graduated from high school with a 1.77 grade point average. For the next several years, Rudy changed his focus from one thing to another. He tried attending junior college for one semester, but flunked every class. He went to work for two years at the local Commonwealth Edison power plant in Joliet—what he considered to be the ultimate dead end job. He even did a two-year hitch in the navy, which turned out to be a turning point for him. That's where he discovered he wasn't dumb and that he could handle responsibility.

After his military service, he returned to Joliet and again worked in the power plant. He was more determined than ever to go to Notre Dame, despite the criticism of his family, friends and coworkers. He knew he was not a failure, and he would find a way to go to South Bend. If you saw the movie, you know that Rudy eventually made it. He quit his job, moved to South Bend and managed to get into Holy Cross College, a community college affiliated with the university. He attended the college for two years and earned a 4.0 average every semester before Notre Dame accepted him. He entered his dream school at age twenty-six, eight years after graduating from high school.

Never let someone else determine your worth.

With two years of sports eligibility remaining, he went out for football. He made the team as a scrub—one of the warm bodies put into practice to keep the good players sharp. But Rudy made the most of it. He worked hard and, after a year, he went from the bottom of the scrubs all the way up to sixth string—the top of the scrubs. His last year, he worked hard again. In the final game of his final season, Rudy lived his dream by getting to play. In the movie, Rudy Ruettiger gets in for only one play at the end of the game, and he sacks the quarterback. But that's not how it really happened. "In real life, I had two chances to get the quarterback," says Rudy. "The first play, I didn't get there in time. I was too anxious and didn't execute the play. I failed."

But once again, Rudy didn't let his failure make *him* a failure. "I knew this was the best chance I would ever get," he explains. "When they snapped the ball, I wasn't worried about failing. I'd done that already, and I knew why I had failed. That's how you eliminate that fear. You keep learning until you have the confidence to perform when you have to. When they snapped the ball for the last time, I put the moves I'd rehearsed in my mind on the guy over me and I got the quarterback." Overjoyed, the team carried him off the field in celebration. Today Rudy is a motivational speaker. And believe it or not, he was the force behind making the movie *Rudy*. Of course, it wasn't easy for him. It took six years to see that happen. (Two years less than it took him to get to Notre Dame!) The people in Hollywood told him, "You're not Paul Horning or Joe Montana." Rudy agreed. "There's only one of them," he explained. "There are a million of me."

You keep learning until you have the confidence to perform when you have to.

That's the great thing about Rudy's story. He didn't have the athletic ability of Michael Jordan. Nor was he the genius of Mozart, Van Gogh, Edison or Einstein. He was just a regular person—like you and me. The only reason he became an achiever instead of average is that he learned to accept life on life's terms and refused to let failure get the better of him. He learned that life presents you with challenges and life's terms may not be your terms, but to succeed you learn to negotiate the terms you have been given.

To be an achiever instead of average, you must learn to accept life on life's terms and refuse to let failure get the better of you.

Rudy's story also emphasizes another very important point. Mistakes really do pave the road to achievement. Leadership expert Peter Drucker said, "The better a man is, the more mistakes he will make, for the more new things he will try. I would never promote to a top-level job a man who was not making mistakes…otherwise, he is sure to be mediocre." My mother has repeatedly told me, "Every test that comes your way will push you toward greater maturity." I vividly remember her response to me when I was in ninth grade and wanted to quit in the middle of the basketball season because I wasn't getting to play. She said, "Your failure will not be that you never got to play. It will be that you simply quit." Funny thing about that lesson I learned in ninth grade. It stayed with me and helped me persevere at times when I wanted to quit the most.

A few years ago I spoke at an event and shared the platform with some very distinguished speakers. One of them however, like me, was really not a well-known celebrity, but was hired because of the strong message he delivered. In the midst of his speech he shared something called *"Autobiography in Five Short Chapters."* As I listened to this speaker, my thoughts were directed toward my wife and some of the friendships she struggled with when we first met. As stated earlier, mistakes do pave the way to achievement. However, sometimes you have to head in a different direction in order to find the pot of gold at the end of the rainbow. Better than anything else, this describes the process of exiting and finding a new direction that can lead to more enriching experiences.

Chapter 1. I walk down the street. There is a deep hole in the street. I fall in. I am lost. I am helpless. It isn't my fault. It takes forever to find a way out.

Chapter 2. I walk down the street. There is a deep hole in the street. I pretend I don't see it. I fall in again. I can't believe I am in the same place, but it isn't my fault. It still takes a long time to get out.

Chapter 3. I walk down the same street. There is a deep hole in the street. I see it there. I still fall in. It's a habit. My eyes are open. I know where I am. It is my fault. I get out immediately.

Chapter 4. I walk down the same street. There is a deep hole in the street. I walk around it.

Chapter 5. I walk down another street.

The only way to go a different direction and see the new territory of achievement and possibilities is to take full responsibility for yourself and your mistakes. Success on any major scale requires you to take responsibility. In the final analysis, the one quality that all successful people have is the ability to take on responsibility. My wife, whose eyes were opened, continued to walk down the same street and even walked around the "deep holes" in her friendships. It wasn't until she took responsibility and walked down another street that she truly discovered how enriching a friendship could be.

The one quality that all successful people have is the ability to take on responsibility.

Another hurdle in accepting life on life's terms is your ability to let go of the past. Someone who is unable to get over previous hurts and failures is held hostage by the past. The baggage you carry around makes it very difficult to move forward and accept the current challenges life puts in your way. In fact, the two things that inhibit you from moving beyond your past are resentment and regret. Resentment is about another person and regret is about you. Unfortunately for you, the person you hold resentment against isn't even bothered by it. Yet, it eats away at you. As for regret, it is about, in most cases, the things you haven't done rather than the things you have done. I have yet to meet a successful person who is balanced and happy who continually dwells on his past difficulties. Of course the lesson my mom has always taught (preached) is to let go and let God. Please read the next sentence carefully. I am in no way making light of a person's past tragedies. People lose children, spouses, parents and friends. They contract cancer and other debilitating diseases. But tragedies don't have to stop a person from possessing a positive outlook, being productive and living life to the fullest.

The baggage you carry around makes it very difficult to move forward and accept the current challenges life puts in your way.

In order to accept today's challenges, you have to get over your past difficulties. When I hear leaders continually talk about how much harder they've had it than anyone else, chances are, they are allowing themselves to be held hostage by their past. I used to report to a person who spent more time *comparing* than conquering. Even in his personal life, he spent all of his energy trying to keep up with the "Joneses." My theory: Never try to keep up with the "Joneses." Drag them down to your level. It's cheaper. The airline industry is a great example of people who live in the past. On numerous occasions, I have overheard airline employees discussing the way it used to be and how much tougher it is today. Even as I sit here and write this sentence, I am on a flight from Dallas to Charlotte listening to a flight attendant in the galley talk (whine) to a passenger about how nice it used to be and how much harder they have it now. The choice is simple. You can learn to accept today's challenges and enjoy the ride, or you can choose to continue comparing today with yesterday and be negative because life is so much tougher.

In order to accept today's challenges, you have to get over your past difficulties.

Another characteristic of people trapped by their past is rationalization. Some people live their entire lives believing that there are good reasons not to get over past difficulties. We now live and work in a society where it is easier to be a victim than to take responsibility. People never find solutions to their problems because they are constantly rehashing the reason they are where they are and, in most cases, are blaming someone else. For years I blamed other people for all the problems I encountered. I know people that have been divorced for ten years and continue to blame their ex-spouse for their problems today. Some people look for reasons to rationalize their behavior and never accept the fact that they are in control and have the option to *walk down another street*. Excuses, no matter how strong, never lead to achievement.

*Some people live their entire lives
believing that there are good reasons
not to get over past difficulties.*

As I mentioned, significant hindrances to living life in the present are resentment and regret. They sap one's energy and leave little that enables them to do anything positive. Regret usually ends up at a pity party. The pity party guest list is usually the same no matter who is throwing the party.

* The Ouldas —Woulda, Coulda, Shoulda

* The Opportunities—Missed and Lost

* The Excuses—Don't Blame Me, Couldn't Help It, It's Their Fault

* The Promises—Broken and Shattered

* The Yesterdays—Too many to count

If you find yourself getting ready to throw a pity party, realize that one person has the power to send all the guests home and break up the party—you. Recognize it's a party you throw yourself, and you can cancel it at anytime. I often remind leaders that if they begin feeling sorry for themselves, it will become very lonely at the top. If it becomes lonely at the top, it is usually a sign no one is following you. Leaders who spend too much time in the past never return to the present and welcome the new day and all it offers. In addition, people who don't get beyond the problems or pain of the past eventually become bitter.

*If it becomes lonely at the top, it is
usually a sign no one is following you.*

On a flight from Charlotte to San Francisco, I sat beside Patricia, an overworked healthcare professional who cried when she began talking about how she let her new boss get the best of her. It was apparent to me, just from sitting beside her, that she was passionate, loving and kind. I also concluded that she was the kind of person you would enjoy working with. Her emotion on the plane that day was due to the fact that she couldn't see the inevitable consequences of not processing old injuries. I reminded her that she did not have to remain the victim of this past encounter with her boss. People become prisoners of their own emotions and allow the past to hold them hostage. No matter what you've experienced, there are people who have had it better than you and have done worse. There are people who've had it worse than you and have done better. The circumstances really have nothing to do with you getting over your personal history. Past hurts can make you bitter or better—the choice is yours. I am happy to report that months later I received an email from Patricia with a glowing report that confirmed she had let go of the past encounter and was passionately moving forward.

*People become prisoners of their own emotions
and allow the past to hold them hostage.*

Every major difficulty you face in life will test your ability to accept life on life's terms. As a leader, you will face numerous unfair experiences. Another great lesson you can learn from my mother is to use turning points (significant changes) in your life to make you a better person. Job losses, divorce, financial setbacks, health problems and even the death of loved ones can provide perspective. It is this perspective that allows you to view major changes within the larger framework of your lifetime and let the healing power of time prevail. In my own personal and professional life, I have had several major turning points that have helped me grow at a deeper level in my career and life. As I have stated to thousands of people who have heard me speak, "One of the key ingredients to being successful is our ability to accept life on life's terms." Life's terms will either make you bitter or better—the choice is yours.

The ABCs to "Accepting Life on Life's Terms"

Adversity can make you better if you don't let it make you bitter.

Be willing to push the envelope.

Choose to continue the journey in spite of the detours.

PASS IT ON

If Tomorrow Never Comes

If I knew it would be the last time I would see you fall asleep, I would tuck you in more tightly and pray the Lord your soul to keep.

If I knew it would be the last time I would see you walk out the door, I would give you a hug and kiss and call you back for more.

If I knew it would be the last time I would hear your voice, I would tape each word so I could play them back day after day.

If I knew it would be the last time I could talk to you, I would say "I love you" instead of assuming that you knew.

If I knew it would be the last time I would share your day, I would spend it all with you.

Tomorrow is not promised to anyone and today may be our last.
So if today is my last, please know how much I love you!

DISCOVER THE POWER OF ME

You are everything you choose to be

Y ou cannot move freely, speak freely, act freely or be free unless you are comfortable with yourself. All of the great leaders I know lead with a great sense of intuition. The only times I have made bad business decisions are when I didn't follow my intuition. My mother's favorite phrase has always been, "Let me pray on it." My approach is to pray about it and then sleep on it. For me, doubt normally means don't. Doubt means do nothing until you know what to do. I follow my intuition almost 100% of the time. In today's fast-paced environment, decisions need to be made swiftly and accurately. While many leaders don't talk about it, intuition is a key part of their decision-making process. Once thought of as the domain of a "gifted few," it is, in fact, readily available to all of us and can be an important component in making business decisions, motivating staff, increasing sales, assessing partnerships and predicting industry trends. Not surprisingly, intuition is the secret weapon of many successful leaders.

The only times I have made bad business decisions are when I didn't follow my intuition.

The dictionary defines intuition as "quick and ready insight." Intuition is direct and immediate knowledge. It tells you what you need to know, when you need to know it, providing you with vital and valuable insight into yourself, your children, friends, business associates and the world around you. There are several ways to receive intuitive information. Practice will tell you what works best for you.

Intuition is direct and immediate knowledge that tells you what you need to know when you need to know it.

Intuitive information often comes through your feelings or emotions. You may simply "feel right" about your decision to hire that new employee. Or, conversely, you may experience an unexplained sense of distrust despite an individual's great credentials. When interviewing, I have always relied on my intuition. Your intuition about a person is usually right even as you argue with yourself regarding their impressive resume. As a matter of fact, I no longer look at resumes as a part of the interview process. Think about it. When was the last time you looked at someone's resume and determined they were motivated, driven, reliable and dedicated? Unfortunately, for many leaders, they hire too many people for what they know, going against their intuitive feelings or emotions that are telling them who they really are. Be careful. Too many times we hire people for what they know and eventually want to fire them for who they are. Listen to your intuition. The art of interviewing is based on your ability to interpret answers. Intuition is the key to interpretation.

Too many times we hire people for what they know and eventually want to fire them for who they are.

The Japanese call using intuition "stomach art." We call such a sensation a "gut feeling." For example, you've just been offered a great career opportunity, yet you notice as you are about to accept the position, your body feels heavy and there's a knot in your stomach. Early in my career, I had this feeling of discomfort immediately after being offered a lucrative sales position in a growing company. I struggled for days and finally fell back on my guideline that doubt usually means don't. My mother's advice was always biblical. She would say, "God is not the author of confusion. When you are not sure of something and seemingly confused, you have your answer." Three months after I declined the position, the company filed for bankruptcy. With four sons you learn quickly to go with your "gut feeling" on certain decisions. I have said on several occasions, "I just don't feel good about it." Of course, any child wants the precise reason for your decision. However, sometimes you just have to rely on "stomach art."

Doubt usually means don't.

You may receive a sudden flash of understanding. This is sometimes called the "Eureka" effect. During my days as a salesperson, I was always a national sales leader in my industry. I firmly believe the key to my success was an interesting approach and practice I implemented early in my career. Before I would meet with a client, I would ask my intuition a series of questions. What do I need to know about this company? What is the best way to approach the decision maker? What should I know about who I'm competing against for this sale? What can I do to win this account? As I would sit, with pen in hand, and quiet my thoughts, intuitive answers would come into my mind. In building my business, I employed the same method. Sometimes we don't allow our intuition to help us because we never take the time to quiet our minds and allow our intuitive thoughts to come forth. Intuitive information comes to you most easily when you are in a relaxed state of mind. To get into a receptive mood, put your calls on hold, shut the door, close your eyes and take a few slow, deep breaths. Bring to mind an issue or problem you're trying to solve. Ask your intuition a question about your concerns. You'll get the most helpful information if you can phrase your questions in a way that evokes more than a "yes" or "no" response. Remain in a quiet and receptive state. Intuition is often described as "still and quiet." It doesn't usually answer in a big, booming voice. It is much subtler. Pay attention to any images you receive, words you hear, physical sensations you experience or emotions you feel. These are all the ways that intuition will communicate with you. Write down any impressions you receive. Some people find that intuitive insights will pop in their mind hours after doing this exercise, while they're driving home or preparing dinner.

Sometimes we don't allow our intuition to help us because we never take the time to quiet our minds and allow our intuitive thoughts to come forth.

Another significant problem we face in the discovery process of "me" is ourselves. It took me almost forty years to figure out what my biggest problem was: me. Not until I understood and changed myself did I have a chance at success. My mother would say it a different way. She would say, "If you could kick the person responsible for most of your troubles, you wouldn't be able to sit down for weeks." Television host Jack Paar echoed the same thought. He said, "Looking back, my life seems like one big obstacle race, with me as the chief obstacle." People don't like to admit they need to change. If they are willing to alter a few things about themselves, they are usually cosmetic changes. Some people are not willing to change because they believe they are supposed to pursue a particular course of action, even though it doesn't suit their gifts and talents. Several years ago my cousin married a man whose course of action was to become a preacher. Always believing he "was called" into the ministry, he never wavered from that direction. Twenty-five years later, he has yet to earn a living preaching or lead a church with more than fifteen people. His talents are music and a God-given ability to play the piano. Too often, when we are not working on areas of strength, we do poorly. My mother would say, "God gets blamed for a lot of bad decisions." As Ben Franklin noted, "There are three things extremely hard—steel, a diamond and to know one's self.

If you could kick the person responsible
for most of your troubles, you wouldn't
be able to sit down for weeks.

A program I have delivered to several groups is entitled *Maximizing Your Potential.* A reference I use is the character Jean Valjean in Victor Hugo's *Les Miserables.* In the play, Jean Valjean declared, "It is nothing to die. It is an awful thing never to have lived." To have an opportunity to reach your potential and discover your true power, you must know who you are and face your flaws. A dear friend of mine, Cynthia Karonis, has always jokingly told my wife that I am flawless. I am 100% sure I am not flawless. However, I am also 100% sure I know my flaws and try to face them on a daily basis. Without this, I have no chance of ever maximizing my potential and discovering the power of me. Most people don't look inside themselves for the same reason they are leery of opening a registered letter—they want to avoid the bad news. Many people see all the bad and deny the good, or they see all the good and deny the bad. To reach your potential, you must see both. A big part of this self-discovery is taking responsibility for who you are as a person. As parents, we sometimes instill a thought process in our children that remains with them through their adult years. We all have limitations and must own up to the things we cannot do, should not do and ought not to do. As mentioned earlier, my cousin's husband has never reached his potential because he has always worked outside his gifts. Do what you do well and you will excel. You will only improve if you enthusiastically develop your God-given abilities. Remember to discover the power of me, you first must change yourself.

A big part of this self-discovery is taking responsibility for who you are as a person.

The thing some people may want to change is their view of themselves. My mother has always told me, "Don't take yourself too seriously." When I speak to leaders, I find that many take themselves much too seriously. Of course, that outlook isn't just reserved for leaders. I meet people every day who need to lighten up. No matter how serious your work, there's no reason to take *yourself* too seriously. There is a lot of power in humor and laughter. Comedian Victor Borge said it this way, "Laughter is the shortest distance between two people." As a speaker, I use a lot of humor to drive home a point because I know the bridge it creates in the learning process. When my former secretary, Margaret, died, her husband Frank asked me to speak at her funeral. His only instructions were, "Make them laugh and remember Margaret the way she was. She always hated when people took themselves too seriously and let their positions and egos get in the way." He said, "It is a celebration of her life and that is what I want them to focus on and remember." Over 750 people would pack a church to pay tribute to a woman who taught me to lighten up. It was her, not me, that said we needed to write a line of cards for people in bad relationships. When I asked her why we needed them, she replied, "People who have experienced bad relationships need an outlet to allow them to laugh at themselves." Of course, I obliged and wrote my first card in the line that made her laugh until she cried. The card said on the outside, "I am miserable without you," and on the inside it said, "It's like you're here!" If you tend to take yourself too seriously, give yourself and everyone else around you a break—lighten up! You will create more power of "me" and, in the process, become more resilient.

---

*Laughter is the shortest distance
between two people.*

Some people never *discover the power of me* because they are waiting for success. Are you waiting for success? If you are, it will never arrive. Success is who you are and what you do during each day and night. It is not a reward or destination. Success is a way of traveling, tilling and gardening.

In my book, *Enjoy The Ride*, I expressed my opinion that there are no successful people, only people who enjoy successful moments in time. We hear about them every day.

"He was in the right place at the right time."

"Her timing was perfect."

"It was an idea whose time had come."

"She knows what she wants and goes after it with a passion."

For the most part, these statements apply to others. Rarely do we direct them toward ourselves. But what if we could say proudly and honestly,

"I placed myself at the right place at the right time."

"My timing was perfect."

"It was my idea whose time had come."

"I know what I want and I go after it with a passion."

Timing may not be everything in life, but when it comes to success, it's difficult to think of another single factor that makes or breaks more people. Everything ultimately happens at a point in time, and when the convergence of factors in time is positive, success is unavoidable. I hear people say all the time, "I am waiting for my ship to come in." I believe that these same people would not be any happier or more successful if their ship did come in. You have to be willing to unload your ship when it does come in. If you're not willing, it once again leaves without you. Timing is the number one factor in success or failure. Maybe the best way to see if you have been waiting for success instead of going after it is presented in the following principles.

The Seven Principles of Timing in Your Life

Principle 1: View your successes from the long view of time.

Principle 2: View your failures from the short view of time.

Principle 3: Dreams and goals must be charted in time to be realized.

Principle 4: Your purpose in life will determine how you choose to segment and prioritize your time.

Principle 5: Your sense of responsibility and your integrity keep you concerned with time.

Principle 6: Perseverance maintains you through the passing of time.

Principle 7: Success is sequenced in time.

The next time you hear someone say, "Timing is everything," you may want to remind yourself that it most certainly is. However, you have to prepare yourself to meet opportunities as they become available. Opportunities always look bigger going than coming. Success truly is sequenced in time and to be in the right place at the right time, you have to be ready. Your personal history and point of view (POV) guide you through time and enable you to understand your decisions, beliefs and leadership ability.

Opportunities always look bigger

going than coming.

Your "point of view" can be influenced and a more powerful "me" shaped by doing a self-assessment. A few years ago I had the pleasure of attending a seminar that incorporated an assessment tool that, for the first time, allowed me to see "me as me." I firmly believe it helped authenticate my leadership style and definitely gave me a clearer understanding of my particular views. It also challenged me to find answers to questions I never addressed. The process took me on a journey of self-discovery that, to this very day, allows me to lead with a perspective I do not think I would have gained without the assessment. Earlier in Lesson 4, you read about the advice I gave my wife regarding one of her friendships. This advice was based on a point of view I had developed after answering one of the questions in the self-assessment. *What is the key to a great friendship?* Finding the answer to that question enabled me to later use it in my leadership career. The following assessment is also a great interview tool. It allows you to not only interview yourself, but use some of these questions when interviewing other people to find out who they really are. Answer the following questions, determine who you really are and create a more authentic "you" that will enable you to lead better.

* Who knows you better than anyone?

* Other than family, who are the most important people in your life right now?

* What's the key to a great friendship?

* Who makes you laugh the hardest?

* Do you have a favorite book or author?

* Are you happy with the way you get along with your parents?

* What are five things you couldn't live without?

* What would someone be surprised to learn about you?

* Was your parents' relationship a strong one?

* Which parent were you closer to?

* Do you believe that people can change?

* Do you believe in God? *(You can't ask this during an interview. However, your answer is important, especially if you do believe in God, but your actions don't match your beliefs.)*

* Has life made you more cynical or more hopeful?

* If you could do anything over in your life, what would it be and what would you do differently?

* What are you the most proud of?

* What do you hope to be remembered for?

* What were you like at school?

* What was your first job and how did you get it?

* How did you decide what field to enter?

* Was money a big factor for you?

* Is there anything you think is absolutely crucial to success at work?

* What was the best job you ever had? What was the worst job you ever had?

* Did your career have any major turning points?

* What are the secrets to a good relationship or marriage?

* Do you have any advice about being a good parent?

* How are you like your parents? How are you different?

* Who in your family is most like you?

* What have you always regretted not asking your parents?

* What is the hardest decision you've had to make?

* What is the hardest decision you haven't made? Why?

* What do you consider to be your strongest character traits?

* What traits or habits do you wish you didn't have?

Any way you look at it, discovering the power of "me" requires commitment and honesty. This self-assessment reinforces that commitment. You have to commit to yourself to take the first step and not just read the above questions, but answer them. In my book, *Enjoy The Ride*,

114

I challenged people to live out their own expectations and not someone else's expectations for them. We allow too many people to define us, make our choices and create our "me." The title of this lesson is *The Power of Me*, not *The Power of We*.

We allow too many people to define us,

make our choices and create our "me."

As two brothers entered their adult life, one completed college and became a highly successful lawyer while the other preferred the outdoors and traveled the country working as a park ranger, outdoor tour guide, seasonal crop worker, etc. The lawyer kept asking his vagabond brother to come live in the city, settle down and to pursue a "respectable" career. In an effort to persuade him, he would send his brother a picture of his BMW and write on the back "my car," a picture of his upscale condominium and write on the back "my house," or a picture of his 40-story high-rise office building with "my office" written on the back. The other brother, finally tiring of the nonsense, put an end to the letters when he sent his lawyer brother a poster of the beautiful majestic Grand Teton Mountains in Wyoming. On the back of the poster he simply wrote "my backyard." Actually, both of these men were successful. They just had different objectives for their lives. I suspect that most of us would prefer to follow the life of the brother who had that beautiful majestic view in Wyoming. Message: You have lots of choices. As long as they're honorable, I encourage you to pursue those which fulfill your dreams because you will never be successful or happy pursuing someone else's dreams.

You will never be successful or happy

pursuing someone else's dreams.

You are responsible for you. The world is a reflection of you. The picture you have of yourself is colored by your experiences, your successes and failures, the thoughts you have about yourself and other people's reactions to you. You are what you believe you are. Your power lies in your own self-image. This blueprint will determine exactly how you will behave, who you will mix with, what you will try and what you will avoid. Your every thought and action stem from the way you see yourself. What this means is that you decide your own worth. You have the power to create an incredible "you" and the power to become a great leadership role model that people will want to follow. Speaking of role models—my mother always challenged me to lead like Jesus and make a difference in my life and in the lives of those I influence. Who better to create the *power of me* than Jesus? And, oh yes, *mum's the word*!

The ABCs to
"Discovering the Power of Me"

Always pursue your own dreams.

Be responsible and own up to your choices

Change your view of yourself.

PASS IT ON

Slow Dance

Have you ever watched kids on a merry-go-round
or listened to the rain slapping on the ground?
Ever follow a butterfly's erratic flight,
or gazed at the sun into a fading night?
You'd better slow down, don't dance so fast.
Time is short. The music won't last.
Do you run through each day on the fly?
When you ask, "How are you?" do you hear the reply?
When the day is done, do you lie in your bed
with the next hundred chores running through your head?
You'd better slow down, don't dance so fast.
Time is short. The music won't last.

Ever told your child, "We'll do it tomorrow,"
and in haste not seen his sorrow?
Ever lost touch, let a good friendship die
cause you never had time to call and say, "Hi."
You'd better slow down, don't dance so fast.
Time is short. The music won't last.
When you run so fast to get somewhere,
you miss half the fun of getting there.
When you worry and hurry through your day,
it is like an unopened gift…thrown away.
Life is not a race, do take it slower.
Hear the music before the song is over.

FOCUS ON THE
TOP LINE

*If you take care of people,
the business will follow*

Unlike many leaders, I share a tremendous amount with my employees. I feel everything—from the tribulations of business to the responsibility to people who depend on me to feed their families. Those things are always factors in my decision-making process. As a leader, make sure you understand the lesson my mother taught me very early in life as I pursued my professional endeavors. She said, "If you're a mom or a dad, that's your No. 1 obligation in life." I was very blessed to have employers who were willing, at different times in my career, to give me a lot of flexibility and a lot of opportunities. It would have been easy for me as the owner of the company to do what was right for my own family and not be concerned about anyone else. But I have always felt an obligation to speak up and let others know that it was OK for them to make their family a priority too.

If you're a mom or a dad, that's your
No. 1 obligation in life.

On November 11, 2005, the world lost the greatest management thinker of the last century. Peter Drucker was the guru's guru. Over his 95 prolific years, he was a true Renaissance man. What John Maynard Keynes is to economics or W. Edwards Deming is to quality, Drucker is to management. In 1932, he published a pamphlet that offended the Nazis. The pamphlet was banned and burned. After witnessing the oppression of the Nazi regime, he found great hope in the possibilities of the modern corporation to build communities and provide meaning for the people who worked in them. For the first time in corporate America, some companies actually began to *focus on the top line*, their most appreciable asset—people. It was Drucker who was the first to assert, in the 1950's, that workers should be treated as assets, not as liabilities to be eliminated. He would often say, "Don't ever think or say 'I'. Think or say 'we'." He went on to say, "Effective leaders know they have the authority only because they have the trust of the organization. They understand that the needs and opportunities of an organization come before their own needs." So what do Peter Drucker and my mother have in common? They both believe that you only learn through listening. Peter Drucker may be the man credited with inventing management, but my mother's ideas still matter and will outlive all of us. Just like Drucker, her insights were not backed up by quantifiable research, but she never backed off when it came to how she believed people should be treated. She also would tell you that even though she doesn't know much about reengineering, restructuring, paradigms, ergonomics or even the bottom line, she knows the most important thing about building a business—how to treat people.

> *Effective leaders know they have the authority only because they have the trust of the organization.*

A friend of mine recently accepted a leadership position in a large company in the Pittsburgh area. I caught up with her six weeks into her new job and asked how she liked it. She said, "I have never worked in an environment where the president of the company was so self-absorbed. The president gave me an awful book to read in which the author rants and raves about why you should fire people in the organization who aren't giving 150% continuously. There is no appreciation in this company and your only reward is keeping your job." I reminded her that Ken Blanchard, a favorite author of hers and mine, said, "Don't expect 150% from people, they're only capable of giving 100%. When you get that, be sure to reward them and let them know you appreciate them and they just might want to do it again." A major cause of negative thinking and poor mental health is self-absorption. Selfishness ultimately hurts not only the people around a self-focused person, but also the selfish person himself. Several years ago when I was at the lowest point in my life and felt a nervous breakdown was inevitable, I went to my friend who is a psychiatrist and asked what he recommended. Much to my surprise, he told me to find someone in need and to do something to help that person. He pointed out that most people are too insecure to give anything away. Most people who focus all their attention on themselves feel that they are missing something in their lives, so they're trying to get it back.

Selfishness ultimately hurts not only the people around a self-focused person, but also the selfish person himself.

My former secretary, Margaret, said something I will forever remember and live by. She said, "In order to get them to care, you have to care enough to know and know enough to care." Of course, with Margaret nothing was ever spelled out easily. Just like the parables in the Bible, she would use real life examples to show me the error of my ways. On one occasion she asked me a series of questions about my subordinates and said my answers would speak volumes about my leadership ability. From naming an employee's child to identifying an employee's birthday, she continued asking questions until I got frustrated and asked her the point of her line of questioning. She said, "In order to be a leader, you have to have followers. To have followers, you have to care enough to know and know enough to care. When you care, you know something about the people who report to you. The more you know about them, the more they will see you care and the more they will want to follow. If it is all about self-absorbed Steve, then eventually you will create a climate of negativity and mistrust." Sound familiar? In some leadership circles it is a common theme. As we ushered in the new millennium, the tendency of corporate managers was to reap massive earnings while firing thousands of their workers. Besides being socially and morally wrong, the organizations paid a heavy price for their self-absorption. When you become focused on the bottom line, your tendency is to ignore your most appreciable asset—your people. In your marriage, self-absorption can produce an environment of insecurity, inferiority, inadequacy and insignificance. When one spouse is selfish and self-focused, it inclines the marriage toward failure because it keeps the other spouse in a negative mental rut. Not until you stop focusing on yourself will you ever reach your full potential as a leader. Most importantly, your leadership ability always determines your effectiveness and the potential impact of your organization.

> *When you become focused on the bottom line, your tendency is to ignore your most appreciable asset——your people.*

One evening my search for chocolate chip cookie dough ice cream would change the manner in which we work at Steve Gilliland, Inc. As I entered a supermarket in Lubbock, Texas, I was surprised by the smiles and demeanor of the employees. A cashier who was cleaning up her work area looked up, smiled and said, "Welcome to United Supermarkets." I then encountered a young man who was stocking shelves who stopped, stood up and asked, "Is there anything I can help you find?" I told him I was looking for chocolate chip cookie dough ice cream. He responded, "Follow me and I will take you right to it." As we entered the aisle that housed numerous brands, he offered his personal opinion on which was the best. We both agreed that Ben & Jerry's was our favorite. He then asked my name, patted me on the shoulder and said, "If you need anything else, Steve, I will be back over in aisle three stocking the shelves. Thanks for shopping at United Supermarkets. We appreciate your business." As I approached the register, the same cashier who greeted me was busy talking to a customer as she rang up her grocery order. I was so impressed with her, I waited in her line. When it was my turn she said, "I knew when you walked in here you looked like a man on a mission and I see your mission was ice cream." She asked me if I lived close by, and when she found out I was from North Carolina asked me about the climate, people and terrain. By the time I left the store, I was so impressed that I went back the next day. Subsequently, I would speak at a United Way Kick-Off event at the Lubbock Civic Center and it was there that I told the audience of my wonderful experience with the locally-based supermarket chain, United Supermarkets. Much to my surprise, when I finished speaking, a gentleman approached and thanked me for the accolades regarding United Supermarkets. He then introduced himself as the CEO. As we talked, I couldn't help but ask what the secret to their employee recruiting and development was. He said, "It is simple. When we hire a person to stock the shelves we tell them their number one priority is to make every person that walks through our doors so happy and satisfied that they will come back again and again and tell ten more people about their experience. Then we tell them to stock the shelves when they have time." He said, "The key to our success is that we focus on people and not on tasks." He went on to say, "Too many organizations are process-driven, not purpose-driven." When I launched my full-time speaking career and built our corporation, I built it on the same philosophy I expound to my audiences. If you continually learn more about your company, your industry, your customer and yourself, you will always be a leader. You will be purpose-driven rather than process-driven and you will make a difference.

> *The key to your success will be that you focus on people and not on tasks.*

Some companies start with the right focus and, through time, shift their focus to the wrong thing and eventually pay the consequences. I am always reminded of this every time I drive by one of the nation's largest retail stores. From the very beginning, the focus was on the customer and making sure the customer was satisfied. So evident was this focus, they even made it a part of their store signage—Satisfaction Guaranteed Always! Then came the change in focus—the bottom line. They began aggressively stocking their shelves with brand name items purchased in such bulk it afforded them the opportunity to price them lower. The leverage (muscle) they had over vendors was so great that the vendors were afraid not to meet their price demands for fear of losing the order, revenue and shelf space. This new-found focus would become a philosophy that would lead them to change their store signs to read—Lowest Prices Always! In addition to the outside signage change, the in-store policies were also changed. With the focus on lowest prices and increasing the bottom line, return policies changed and the number of employees was reduced to meet the bottom line goals. The personal service is no longer the norm and people have begun shopping elsewhere. Why? Focus!

---

*We've been all the way to the moon
and back, but we have trouble crossing
the street to meet a new neighbor.*

As a nation, our focus has changed. It is the paradox of time. The paradox of time in history is that we

Have taller buildings, but shorter tempers
Wider freeways, but narrower viewpoints
We spend more, but have less
We buy more, but enjoy it less

We have bigger houses and smaller families

Bigger churches and smaller congregations

A multitude of prayers, but very little faith

A blessed life, but lack of gratitude

A loving God for our blemished hearts

We have more conveniences and less time

We have more degrees, but less sense

More knowledge, but less judgment

More experts, but more problems

More medicine, but less wellness

We have multiplied our possessions,
but reduced our values

We talk too much, love too seldom and hate too often

We've learned how to make a living, but not a life

We've added years to life, not life to years

We've been all the way to the moon and back,
but we have trouble crossing the street
to meet a new neighbor

We've conquered outer space, but not inner space

We've cleaned up the air, but polluted the soul

We've split the atom, but not our prejudice

We have higher incomes, but lower morals

We've become long on quantity, but short on quality
These are the times of tall men and short character
Steep profits and shallow relationships
More leisure, but less fun
More kinds of food, but less nutrition

These are the days of two incomes, but more divorce
Of fancier houses, but broken homes
It is a time when there is much in the show window
And nothing in the stock room
A time when technology can bring a letter to you
And a time when you can choose to make a
difference or just hit delete.

People now have hearts motivated by self-interest. Servant leadership is one of the hottest topics in leadership circles. As you consider where your focus is, ask yourself this question. "Am I a servant leader or a self-serving leader?" Too many times our own agendas, status and gratification come ahead of anything else. It has become rather fashionable in leadership circles to talk about the concept of servant leadership. The concept suggests that inherent in the act of leadership is the natural desire and corresponding choice to first serve others. The defining element lies in a person's first inclination. Is it to lead or is it to serve? The first inclination of great leaders is servanthood. Most people are drawn to leadership because they feel compelled to serve a purpose larger than themselves.

Am I a servant leader

or a self-serving leader?

Some people are uncomfortable with the idea of servant leadership. They may see it as oppressive. For others who have been conditioned to view leadership as a tough, macho thing, servant leadership may seem submissive or weak. Despite its alien feel, servant leadership is a form of leadership particularly well suited to today's business world. First, servant leadership sets people free. Stop! Some of you who are reading this need to read the next few sentences slowly and carefully. Servant leadership means helping people remove the obstacles in their way and helping them acquire the tools they need to do their jobs better. It doesn't mean saying you will be there for them, then becoming the largest obstacle in their way. It means jumping into the trenches and being willing to do whatever you ask of others. Think about it. There is a sense of significance and a feeling of accomplishment when you know you've played a small part in lightening the load of a colleague who is overwhelmed. The acts of servant leadership are dignifying, not demeaning. Having worked for someone who always preached servant leadership, but never practiced it, I can attest to how demoralizing it can be. Like anything else, you can't read books on the subject and hang posters in the building and expect people to buy into your leadership style. You have to practice what you preach. Leadership is being a faithful, devoted, hard-working servant of the people you lead and participating with them in the agonies as well as the ecstasies of life. When I founded Steve Gilliland, Inc., I was determined to make sure everything I did inspired motivation in the employees I would hire.

FOCUS ON THE TOP LINE

Leadership is being a faithful, devoted, hard-working servant of the people you lead and participating with them in the agonies as well as the ecstasies of life.

The role of leadership is to protect the sources of motivation and draw upon them to invigorate and revitalize people who temporarily lose hope. This synergy is gained through commitment, honor and beliefs. Commitment creates meaning in one's work and it is meaningful work that motivates someone to be productive. I will always remember coaching junior high football and realizing that everyone wanted their son to be the quarterback, running back or wide receiver. Playing on the line was not a meaningful experience to an eighth grader. After all, who did the cheerleaders want to date? It was only when I created meaning for their position, gave them a "nickname" and changed the award from MVP (Most Valuable Player) to MVL (Most Valuable Lineman) that the players realized the significance of their position. Just like junior high football players, people are moved to higher levels of motivation when work is no longer seen as a vocation, but an avocation.

Commitment creates meaning in one's work and it is meaningful work that motivates someone to be productive.

You also have to raise people to higher levels of motivation by showing them how their individual contributions are linked to the major purpose of the organization. This is done by acknowledging people's contributions in various ways. In junior high football, every time we scored a rushing touchdown, the linemen were given the same "bulldog" sticker to place on the back of their helmet that the running back was given. In practice we would meticulously show how one block from a lineman was the key to the entire play. Many times we would remove one of the linemen from a play and only have four of them instead of five. The point we made was very impacting. Every individual person has a contribution that is linked to the purpose and success of the team. Every play is designed for a touchdown based on individual contributions. Leaders need to use just about any means available to show people the importance of what they do. As a result, people begin to see how they can make a difference. People become energized when they understand the significance of their contributions. It activates within them an inner drive to contribute more.

Every individual person has a contribution that is linked to the purpose and success of the team.

When people believe in you, they help you blossom. They help you become a bigger, stronger, more capable person. Leaders show their belief in people by giving them assignments that are often way outside the boundaries of their normal job descriptions. Most organizations think you have to have an expertise in something before you can become a leader. Motivation comes from showing people that you believe in them. The key is for you to place people where they can have a positive impact and grow. Too many times we hire the right people, but we place them in the wrong positions. As a leader, it is your responsibility to acknowledge the gifts people bring to the table and then help them apply those gifts.

As a result, the impact of their gifts expands because they use them more frequently and more effectively.

Motivation comes from showing people that you believe in them.

If you are interested in focusing on the top line, consider the following. These five things will help you expand your scope of influence and deepen the relationship you need with the people who contribute to your bottom line. *Walk your talk.* You expand your influence in an organization when people believe that you can be trusted and that you are credible. Integrity means being the person you say you are. *Focus on things you can control.* You have a choice every day to either complain about what you can't control or focus on what you can. As a leader, you will make more things happen by focusing on what you can control. *Be prepared.* I firmly believe the success of our company is based on the premise that we do more research than most people in our industry. We take pride in making sure we are on the cutting edge of information, technology and trends. *Love people into action.* Love conquers the defensiveness that closes people to influence. When people feel loved, the walls come down. People don't care how much you know until they know how much you care. Love is a source of influence. *Listen for more than you hear.* Over the years, I have discovered that listening is powerful because it shows a genuine desire to understand the unique needs and feelings of others. At the beginning of this book, I acknowledged Sharon Alberts. Her gift is listening to people and hearing what they say. Her open door policy is more than words. It is a commitment and sincere desire to hear what people have to say. Her availability and willingness to listen to everyone within her organization, no matter what position they hold, is a tribute to her success. Her ability to listen always evokes some type of action or emotional response which essentially shows people that they have been influential. More importantly, these people know that the company's senior leadership will be influenced by what they hear. People who feel they have been heard are more willing to hear others.

Listening is powerful because it shows a genuine desire to understand the unique needs and feelings of others.

The choice is yours and the time is now. There will always be people who will criticize you for daring to be authentic and caring about people more than you care about your position. Dealing with people issues is often messy and complex. I suspect this is why many leaders tend to focus on the bottom line and approach people as replaceable and more of a means to an end rather than as the real reason for their success. When you begin to realize that people are your most appreciable asset, you will have unveiled the secret for successful leadership. A lesson you can ill afford not to learn. Take care of your top line!

The ABCs to "Focusing on the Top Line"

Appreciate people.
Believe in people.
Care about people.

PASS IT ON

Provision Principles

If you want *confidence*—provide **encouragement**.

If you want *appreciation*—provide **praise.**

If you want *self-esteem*—provide **approval**.

If you want *love*—provide **acceptance**.

If you want *generosity*—provide **sharing**.

If you want *truth*—provide **honesty**.

If you want *risk takers*—provide **security**.

BE OF SOUND
MIND AND BODY

The greatest wealth is health.

I learned something when my father died in November, 2004. I suppose it's true with any person you've been a part of for more than four decades, but I am still struck by the fact that he is no longer with us. While there are situations you cannot control, it's your privilege to take charge of what you can. This final lesson is one that my mother lives and breathes. A diabetic, she is the epitome of a person who sacrifices to stay physically fit (healthy diet, exercise, plenty of sleep, etc.). What happened to my father? When did he lose his health and vitality? His lack of self-mastery, combined with his inability to find balance, never allowed him the opportunity to handle the competing responsibilities he faced in his late sixties. Leaders who neglect their own health and well-being for "the sake of the job" often sabotage their own success over the long term. I, myself, have fallen prey and become apathetic toward my own physical well-being. My energy, vibrancy, style and presence are intimately connected to my physical well-being. Regardless of their leadership area, leaders need to realize they represent a successful life when they lead others.

Leaders who neglect their own health and well-being for "the sake of the job" often sabotage their own success over the long term.

Every year on March 4th (March Forth) our company, Steve Gilliland, Inc., is closed. This is a paid holiday for all employees to remind them how important it is to *be of sound mind and body*. We, like many companies, begin our fiscal year energized and ready to implement the strategies and tactics necessary to achieve our goals. We aim for excellence and are driven by the vision of our accomplishments. But, as a friend of mine once said, "Even the best have to rest." We arrive early, skip lunch, work late and grab a fast-food sandwich on the run. Even worse, we unwind with a glass of wine, believing it will relax us. However, it slows our metabolism and inhibits our digestive process—a process necessary for our health and well-being. As leaders, we need to learn what we teach others. We preach discipline and teach the value of making the right choices, yet we fail to find ways to be healthy. Edward Stanley, Earl of Derby, 1873, said, "Those who think they have no time for bodily exercise will sooner or later have to find time for illness." For our employees, *March Forth* is a time of renewal and reminder. Ironically, it also is the time of year when most people have already given up, or are in the process of giving up, on their resolution to diet, exercise and lose weight. I write from experience.

As leaders, we need to learn
what we teach others.

How can you be the best you can and celebrate your efforts in pursuing excellent health habits without getting defeated because you are not perfect? Stop aiming for perfection! If you find that you're not as healthy and fit as you'd like to be, it may be because you're aiming for perfection, telling yourself that you'll eat 100 percent healthy meals all the time, exercise for an hour daily and always get the right amount of sleep. But you rarely follow through. If you are like me, you feel that if you can't do it perfectly, you don't bother with good health habits at all. Health and well- being are not skills. They are a state of mind. By writing this book and reminding myself of my mother's lessons, I have since kicked myself in the back side and elevated my health habits to a level that will maintain my health and vitality for years to come.

Health and well-being are not skills.
They are a state of mind.

I have presented a keynote speech entitled *What to Say When You Talk to Yourself* numerous times and always wondered the same thing. Do people who hear it actually realize that the chatter in their head is either something you ignore or listen to? I catch myself driving down the road with the radio on, but I'm not really hearing it. It's more background noise than music. The same can be said of our self-talk. What we say when we talk to ourselves is extremely important because it can either change our thinking or cause us to learn from it. The better you get at catching your negative, perfectionist self-talk tendencies, the sooner you will enjoy the efforts you put into your healthy lifestyle habits. Instead of the negative self-defeating comment, "What good will twenty minutes do on this treadmill? I need twenty hours on it!" you could say, "I would like to go for more than twenty minutes, but I challenged myself while I was doing it. That is far better than no activity at all."

What we say when we talk to ourselves is extremely important because it can either change our thinking or cause us to learn from it.

I have always said, "Comparison prohibits you from seeing your uniqueness." In this book let me add, "It also prohibits you from looking inside. When we look outside at the people around us, we are not able to realistically reflect on what we want to accomplish in our exercise and nutrition program. Again, we aim for perfection, or someone else's definition of what they think is best for us. My best friend is extremely health conscious and, at age 50, looks like he is 35. His energy level and vitality are at a level most people only dream about (me included). What's wrong with that? Nothing, as long as your body, lifestyle, support systems and available time to exercise are the same as his. Look inside, not outside, to determine how much, how often and with whom you'll pursue health and fitness. Your career, travel and personal relationships are uniquely your own. Determine how to take care of your needs to fit your seasons of life and your style preferences. Ask a professional if you are unsure what is truly healthy for your body. Exercise on your own terms, in your own way and acknowledge when you're actually doing your best and when you're not. So often we lie to ourselves about how much effort we make to exercise and usually it comes down to us excusing it because of time. We will read the newspaper and check our personal email every day, but we can't find twenty minutes to exercise. We say we want balance in our lives, but we contradict our words with our actions. If you do not become passionate about your physical well-being, you will never truly achieve it.

Look inside, not outside, to determine
how much, how often and with whom
you'll pursue health and fitness.

Speakers, preachers, physicians and people from every walk of life have an opinion on balancing life's issues, reducing stress and taking care of your well being. For me it comes down to passion. Our tendency will be to focus on and do more of what we are passionate about. People who carve up their day into pieces (like a pie) are the most susceptible to being unbalanced. A schedule of activities to fit everything into a day may on paper seem like balance. However, when you come right down to it, passion is what moves you forward and keeps you going. Balance is not about compartmentalizing our lives. It is more about passion. It is passion that gets us back on the bike after we crash. You simply can't lead a crashless life as an entrepreneur and leader. What fears stand in your way? Your well-being is important. You realize what it is and yet remain paralyzed regarding situations that are within your control. For some of you, it is a question of balance. You have been so busy trying to balance your life that you have missed one huge point. Balance means equilibrium, which is the absence of external forces influencing the status quo. If that sounds kind of dreary, consider this. To balance a bicycle, you have to have forward movement. Hence, I tend to distort the traditional meaning of balance to instead imply progress. I don't regard staying on the bike as success. If you're not falling from time to time or not crashing into something because you are going a tad too fast on the turns, then you're not leading, you're just maintaining.

To balance a bicycle, you have to have forward movement.

When I began my professional speaking career, I did nothing but contract work for a seminar company. I thoroughly enjoyed the speaking, but was always troubled by the number of days I spent away from home. 125-150 dates a year, combined with travel days, meant I was gone almost 250 days a year. I attended a convention and was asked by another speaker what my fee was. When I told him, he simply said, "Why not double, triple or quadruple your fee, break out on your own and spend less time traveling? You will make more money, be challenged to take your career to another level and, in the process, place less strain on yourself physically." Backpedaling from him I responded, "I could never charge that amount." The problem was that if I actually believed that statement, then I was right. But that belief system was based on balance, not passion. I didn't want to rock the boat and watched dozens of other speakers trapped in the same thing I was. We all had no forward movement! The bicycle we were all on was really a treadmill. If I had passion, I would have believed more in my value, increased my fees, provided products for passive income and so on. Instead, I was afraid the bike might actually move. Passion provides freedom. I love what I do and I know how I am doing. I don't need people to tell me that I am the greatest speaker who ever lived and that I've changed the lives of their entire community. Stop worrying about balance and start focusing on becoming passionate about your mental and physical well-being. You don't ride a bike with balance if you want the ride of your life. You ride it with passion. If you want to be of sound mind and body, then get on the "bicycle of well-being" and begin pedaling your way to a healthier happier life.

Passion provides freedom.

Recognize that your health, strength, endurance, body composition and flexibility will change over time. Do the best you can each day to be active, eat well, rest and connect with others. As long as you are patient with the process and don't take radical or unrealistic shortcuts, your body and mind will benefit. During a span of five years, I personally tried the Atkins diet, the South Beach diet and my own version of the two. I lost 25—30 pounds each time and yet, at the end of five years, weighed the same as when I started. Although I lost weight, I never truly changed my eating habits long term. I know I am about to upset the diet experts, but the Atkins diet and South Beach are radical and unrealistic. They both starve your body of important nutrients and high percentages of people who attempt them usually fail. A patient process of eating less, reducing the intake of fat and sugars and exercising moderately will enable you to gradually lose weight and, most importantly, keep it off because you changed your long-term eating habits. Health and energy are wonderful rewards in themselves. While you want to be patient with yourself, you also want to be proactive. When I began to put as much effort into my physical well-being as I did my presentations, I became healthier. As you discipline yourself to make healthier choices, remember the benefit of wellness goes beyond weight and energy. You will likely become more patient, creative and relaxed.

Health and energy are wonderful
rewards in themselves.

Consistent physical activity is the greatest gift you can give yourself as a leader. Making time to exercise is both a privilege and a challenge. Different seasons of life, crisis, energy level changes, health challenges and career changes can interrupt the flow of your healthy routines. Instead of putting your head down and barreling through and berating yourself for not doing more, look up and be grateful for what you can do. I personally can't jog because of my knees. For years I used this as an excuse for not exercising. When I began to consider what was in my control, I purchased a great pair of walking shoes and began the process. The walks that are now a passionate part of my day help me celebrate my energy level and reduce the feelings of stress in my life. The best thing you can do for yourself as a leader is to ensure that you are both physically and mentally ready to lead others. My mother always taught me to take care of my body because of the strategic connection it has to your mind. You only need to meet my mother to appreciate how her healthy habits keep her mind sharp. She has more energy than most people do in their forties.

The best thing you can do for yourself as a
leader is to ensure that you are both physically
and mentally ready to lead others.

The next time you find yourself frustrated, fatigued or stressed, stop and consider the truth of your circumstances. Your leadership success is determined by the decisions you make on a daily basis. If you are not doing your best to make small, healthy decisions, choose differently. Daily moment-to-moment choices create balance and well-being. Put the same level of enthusiasm and passion into taking care of yourself as you do your clients. I have had people stop me after a speaking engagement and tell me they could feel the energy in the building as they walked out. I then said to myself, "I wonder what my health would be like if I developed a similar level of passion and enthusiasm for my self-care?" As a leader, you strive to make a difference in people's lives while making a profit. Yet, without first making a positive difference in your own health and well-being, you limit your impact and increase the wear and tear on your health and relationships. Excellent health habits focus on the small choices that make a big difference. Performing well as a leader presupposes you do the very best to maintain and develop the most important tool in your profession—you!

> *Your leadership success is determined by the decisions you make on a daily basis. If you are not doing your best to make small, healthy decisions, choose differently.*

The following action steps will help you stay more balanced in your personal and professional life.

* Be sure to adapt an "I can and will do this" attitude. Be feisty in your approach to your health.

* (write it down) your exercise time daily no matter how brief the time. ten minutes is better than nothing.

* Purchase exercise clothes, including shoes, that are comfortable and motivate you to keep a regular exercise schedule. If you travel, pack them!

* Purchase CDs and DVDs that will inspire, relax or challenge you. When you stop learning, you stop leading.

* Purchase a noise-canceling headset. It will eliminate noise and reduce stress on your body and mind.

* Have an accountability partner who will challenge you to greater self care. Exercise or walk together and encourage each other along the way.

* Get a baseline physical with a complete blood workup so you can benchmark changes. *On June 14, 2002, I had a heart attack. When I look back, I remember thinking how stupid it was to be so successful and come so close to giving it up because of my health.*

* Ask this question frequently: "Will this choice (regarding food, rest, a phone call, another meeting) bring me closer to or take me further away from my goals for great well-being?"

Good health is your birthright. By good health, I mean energy and vitality. It is your right to wake each morning with the confidence that your body can more than just "struggle through." Too many people have the notion that good health means a mere absence of disease. If we look at the mind-body connection, it is easy to see how much our body is affected by our mental state. Our subconscious mind is monitoring our healing process every second of the day. Your body is continually rebuilding and its rebuilding blueprint comes from your mind. When your wounded finger heals, what controls the building of the new cells? What intelligence is it that ensures that when you lose a finger nail, it is another finger nail you grow on the end of your finger and not a bladder? Something has to be controlling all these things! Let us not take the miracle of our physical being for granted!

Your body is continually rebuilding and its rebuilding blueprint comes from your mind.

At the beginning of this lesson, I said the following regarding my mother and her health. She is the epitome of a person who sacrifices to stay physically fit (healthy diet, exercise, plenty of sleep, etc.). The checklist above is a pretty accurate glimpse into her secret for well-being. To say she is feisty about her commitment to health is an understatement. When I visit, she is always reminding me of what I should be eating. Of course, her favorite line is, "Stephen, you look tired. Are you getting enough sleep?" She then reminds me that no matter how successful you are, it is all for naught without your health.

> *No matter how successful you are,*
> *it is all for naught without your health.*

Besides healthy diet, exercise and plenty of sleep, you need to take time to rest. I am always reminded by my technological ineptness that sometimes you don't have to replace any parts on your computer to have it work better. You just have to reboot it. Earlier in this lesson, I mentioned that our employees celebrate *March Forth*. As a leader, I encourage you to "reboot" your computer (you) and take time to simply rest. With my busy travel schedule (over 150,000 air miles each year), office responsibilities and personal things I enjoy (my wife and children), it is a high priority of mine to "reboot" every week. I have started to do something that I recommend to every leader who faces the challenges of today and the uncertainty of tomorrow—take one hour every week to rest. No travel, no office, no wife, no children, no book, no reading material, no newspaper—just you, alone, for one hour at your favorite place to unwind. Maybe it is your corner pub, a park near your home or my personal favorite, Panera Bread in Clemmons, North Carolina. Once a week I go to Panera Bread, get a fresh cup of coffee (or three) and just sit, relax and think. As a professional speaker and author, I find myself getting recharged and actually raising the bar on my creativity and thought process. I love my wife more than words can express. However, I go by myself with nothing but my thoughts. It is there I also have some of my best talks with God. No schedule, no work, no deadline, no decisions and, most importantly, no stress—unless how much half and half to put in your coffee is stress.

To every leader who faces the challenges
of today and the uncertainty of tomorrow—
take one hour every week to rest.

To be of sound mind and body requires that you take care of your mind and body. Just like your car, your mind and body require regular maintenance to keep them running smoothly. I remember hearing a speaker talk about what he did to stay sharp on the platform. He said, "As a father, husband, business leader and speaker, I spend quiet time every week to ensure I don't burn out and unravel. I can't afford to let any of my responsibilities suffer so I continually take time to relieve my stress through scheduled quiet time." He went on to explain that he had a favorite booth at a diner where he would go and simply have a glass of sweet tea, a piece of peach pie and do nothing but sit and relax. No cell phone, reading material or work of any kind. He also said, "In the two years since I have been doing this, some of my most creative and productive thoughts have been born during these times."

Just like your car, your mind and body
require regular maintenance to
keep them running smoothly.

On November 23, 2004, I was abruptly reminded of how fragile life really is. How can you be the point guard on your state championship basketball team (age 17), the captain of your corporate golf team (age 28), the president of the local little league (age 37), the commander of your local VFW Post (age 47), the driver for the Harlem Globetrotters (age 66) and die (age 72)? The truth: my father, Floyd Lewis Gilliland, disregarded every piece of advice you have just read in this lesson. Although warned several times, he approached life as if he were invincible. As a leader, I can't emphasize this final lesson enough. You can either live to work or work to live. You can starve your mind and body of the ingredients necessary to enjoy both your professional life and your personal life. Too many times we spend all of our energy at work only to arrive home exhausted with nothing left to give to our loved ones. You can read a lot of books on leadership that challenge your thinking. You can adapt numerous ideas to become a better leader (Lessons 1—7 in this book), but without your mind and body performing at a peak level, you will never truly accomplish everything you could. So I challenge you. Begin today to live a healthier life by being of sound mind and body. I guarantee you will become a better leader at work and at home…and be much happier in the process.

The ABCs to "Being of Sound Mind and Body"

Adapt an "I can and will" attitude.

Balance yourself by moving forward.

Choose where you want to be.

PASS IT ON

21 Easy Ways to Improve Your Diet

* Have seconds on vegetables. Doing so will help ensure you consume the recommended three to five servings per day. Reminder: A typical vegetable serving size is 1/2 cup.

* Eat a whole-grain cereal for breakfast.

* Top your cereal with fresh fruit. You'll add fiber and, depending on the fruit, a healthy dose of vitamins A, B and C.

* Order healthy choices when you eat out. Request foods such as fish and chicken that are baked instead of fried.

* Keep salads healthy by going easy on regular dressing or using low-fat or non-fat dressing. Four tablespoons of regular dressing can contain 60 grams of fat, which is as much as most adults should consume in a day.

* Eat fish for dinner at least once a week. The omega-3 fatty acids in fish can reduce your risk of heart attack.

* Choose fruit over fruit juice. You'll consume less sugar and more fiber.

149

* Add onions to pizza, sandwiches, hamburgers, salads and chili. They're good for your blood and heart.

* Educate yourself about nutrition. Your new knowledge will make it easier to eat a well-balanced diet.

* Drink a full glass of water before a meal and another one with it. You'll stay hydrated and be less likely to overeat.

* Add lentils, beans, kasha, brown rice and peas to your diet for a fiber boost.

* Buy low-fat or fat-free bologna, ham and other cold cuts.

* Choose low-fat alternatives when a craving hits. Go for a low-fat candy bar instead of a regular one, or baked chips instead of regular ones.

* Don't peel apples, pears, peaches and potatoes. Many of their nutrients, and a lot of their fiber, are contained in, or are just under, their skins.

* Buy healthier low-salt versions of soups, pasta, sauces and lunch meats if you're watching your sodium intake.

* Drink iced tea instead of soda. Tea contains antioxidants and can help protect against heart disease and cancer. A 12-ounce can of regular soda contains 10 teaspoons of sugar. Diet sodas are sugar-free, but contain no nutrients and lots of chemicals.

* Read food labels of comparable brands of salad dressings, convenience foods, frozen foods, packaged dinners, cookies and crackers. Choose those with the least fat, cholesterol and sodium.

* Switch from whole milk to 1 percent or skim milk.

* Take fresh or dried fruit to work for a mid-morning or mid-afternoon snack.

* Eat reasonable portions of food. Even healthy foods can cause weight gain if you eat too much of them.

More Lessons
to Consider

*From my wife, my mother, Margaret
and my inner circle of friends*

LESSON 9
Be questioned for who you are,
rather than believed for who you are not.

My mom, being a Baptist, cringes when I tell the joke about the difference between a Baptist and a Methodist—a Methodist will say hello to you in the liquor store. Translation—be true to yourself.

LESSON 10
Like your job. Love your family.

With so many books and articles being written on the differences between the generations (baby boomers, generation X, generation Y), one thing has become perfectly clear to me. There really is life after work. My wife is the one who taught me to schedule my work around my life, not my life around my work. I am very passionate about my job. However, I am very much in love with my family. You can always find work, but you can't replace your family.

LESSON 11
A point of view is worth 80 IQ points.

Margaret, my former secretary, taught me to always let others bring out the best in me. She believed that the more perspective you have on any subject or situation, the better decision you will make. Several perspectives allow me to see things from a variety of viewpoints. Remember—none of us is as smart as all of us.

LESSON 12
You can't change people. You can only influence them.

People never listen to what you say as much as they watch what you do. Unfortunately, your desire to change a person's attitude or behavior is overshadowed by the negative influence you may have. I was always told, "If you want a smile, give one first." Too many times we try to change our employees, our children and our family when the only power we have is to change ourselves and influence them positively.

LESSON 13
A "will be" is a "has been" in progress.

Had I listened to every person in my life who said I couldn't, I would have never left where I was. I consider myself a "has been" who embraced the attitude of "I will be" and "I believe I can" to emerge as a person who "has done it." Our job isn't to judge other people on where they have been, but rather encourage them in what they can become. Everything in life is a process that, through trial and error, helps us progress to the next plateau.

LESSON 14
Abundance is the result of appreciation, not accumulation.

When I was growing up, my mother taught me and my brother a valuable lesson which, at the time, seemed mean and insensitive. Anything we left lying on the floor of our bedroom that was not put away where it belonged was given away to someone less fortunate than we were. She always said, "You will always know you have too much when you no longer appreciate it enough to take care of it."

Lesson 15
When you spend time doing something someone else can do,
you won't have time to do what only you can do.

The greatest lesson in delegation is contained in this lesson. Too many times we spend time attending to things that our employees can do. This leaves us less time to concentrate on the things that only we can do. My staff doesn't write books or speak to an audience. However, if I don't delegate the administrative side of my business to them but try to do it myself, I will never have enough time to write, prepare and deliver the speech.

Lesson 16
Become addicted to continuous self-improvement.

My mother gets credit for my thirst for information and my enjoyment of reading, while my former secretary gets the credit for my addiction to improving in every area of my life. Margaret would say, "The day you stop learning is the day you stop leading." The success of our business has been the recruiting, retention and continuous improvement of our staff. My ability to succeed as a professional speaker is directly related to the new information I take in on a daily basis. I am enrolled in a self-study program entitled "Never Stop Learning."

Lesson 17
Clarity is the perspective you can't see.

The glass is either half empty or half full, depending on whether you are drinking or pouring. I learned early in life that there is no reality, only perspective. What a person sees, or perceives to see, is their reality. In leadership the greatest gift to perspective is clarity. Searching and finding the truth allows you to *gain* a perspective that sometimes eludes us and distorts our reality.

LESSON 18
Compassion gallops. Judgment merely walks.

Rev. Martin Luther King, Jr. once said, "You will never remember the words of your enemies, only the silence of your friends." It never ceases to amaze me when I am around people who delight in another's misery. We are so quick to judge, and yet so slow to reach out. It is much easier to find the fault in someone when it appears they have made a wrong choice. Great leaders not only lead from their heart, they judge by it too.

LESSON 19
Confrontation is a positive way to handle negative events.

Wow! My mother always said, "Behavior not confronted never changes." One of the hardest lessons you will learn is to confront people out of love and a desire to see them get better. Anyone can confront, but doing it out of love is the real challenge. I have met numerous people in leadership positions who get caught up in supervising instead of leading. Supervisors enforce the rules. Leaders help people grow because of them.

LESSON 20
Courage is being scared and then doing
the thing you think you can't do.

Leaving a secure job, becoming a stepfather and writing a book are just a few of the things that were on my list of "can't do's." The thought of raising another person's children never even entered my mind. My fear of failure in my personal and professional life never stopped me from doing what others, and even myself, didn't think I could do. I remember when our company reached its first million dollars in revenue. I took more than a moment to remember how scared I was to leave a great job to go out on my own and start a new business.

LESSON 21
Don't go through life. Grow through life.

It is a fact that when a flower stops growing, it dies. Hmmm. Let's face the facts. Some people wake up every day and just go through the motions. They want more out of life, but are not willing to pay the price of growing to succeed at a higher level. We want nicer cars, houses and vacations, but when it comes to growing, we think there is something called *"Miracle Grow"* for humans. When you stop growing, your spirit dies and your passion ends.

LESSON 22
Follow the talent you have been given.

Credit this lesson to a coach I had in college. He said, "The tragedy of some people is their inability to use to the fullest what they have been given." He always encouraged us to work hard and stay focused on our strengths. He was always preaching that we spend so much time trying to improve our weaknesses that we never totally maximize our strengths. Sounds like great advice for a guy who always wanted to speak in front of people, but pursued everything but that for years.

LESSON 23
Give some people an inch and they think they're a ruler.

Ouch! Mom always warned me about people who were enamored with themselves due to their positions in life. As I travel the world speaking to leaders, I always remind them that if they are all wrapped up in themselves, they are overdressed. As mentioned previously in this book, a great attribute to acquire is authenticity. Power can move mountains and remove leaders.

LESSON 24
To give is better than to receive.

As a professional speaker, it is my job to be center stage, to have a voice, to command attention. As a caring citizen, however, my charge is infinitely different. I have always been impressed by people who live by the words of William Barclay, the popular 20th century Scottish theologian who once said, "Always give without remembering; always receive without forgetting." This is, indeed, the microcosm of giving—to give, not in the spirit of obligation or debt, but merely in the spirit of service.

Parents understand this concept innately, simply in the way they love their children. We love not because the child loves first and deserves to be loved in return, but simply because it's natural for parents to give unconditional love.

Unconditional love and caring are the concepts of stewardship—committing financial, educational, reputational and relational resources to nurture, nourish, guide and grow other people and causes. The investment to give one's self and to share resources is central to the premise of stewardship. It is limited not by the number of available dollars, but only by one's heart, attitude and commitment to effect lasting change.

My friends, we are fortunate. God has blessed us. We have been given many opportunities. However, significance is measured not by our opportunities, but by our choices. Let us choose significance. Let us all choose to give, not merely give back. After all, life is lived best when giving is seen not as an obligation, but as a privilege and a priority.

LESSON 25
Growing up stunts your growth.

From fantasy football to a neighborhood whiffle ball game, I will forever stay the course of having fun and being myself. Even as I write this, I am sitting on an airplane enroute to San Diego wearing my 2005 AFC Conference Championship t-shirt (Pittsburgh Steelers) over my dress shirt. Why? I love the Steelers, they are heading to the Super Bowl and I am proud to be a fan. But what about a potential client I may encounter on a plane? If they're looking for someone who can speak from their heart, then I'm their man. If they're looking for someone who would never be caught dead in a Steelers t-shirt on a flight, then they need to hire a more serious and mature person who can speak from their head and miss the audience's heart.

LESSON 26
I would rather see a sermon than hear one.

Your mother said it too. Your actions will always speak louder than your words. Of course, my mother had a much more flavorful version. She said, "I would rather see a sermon than hear one." Translation—make sure you can walk the talk and set an example of what you expect of other people. How many times have we read about a person who was adamant about something only to contradict themselves with their behavior?

LESSON 27
If you're not serving the customer, serve someone who is.

Sometimes in leadership we get so far removed from the customer that we forget the reason for our success—our front-line people. They make the difference and also have the ability to make an impression that can be long-lasting, either negatively or positively. Organizations like Southwest Airlines are a great example of leadership having learned and applied this lesson. Their success is based on their willingness to serve their employees who, in turn, serve their customers.

LESSON 28
If you don't believe in yourself, very few others will.

People are drawn to confidence. As mentioned earlier, our beliefs drive our expectations. In other words, what you believe, you expect. How you see yourself performing in certain situations is a result of how you believe. What you think, you are. When you lead other people, they need to have a shared sense of beliefs that begins with the way you see yourself.

LESSON 29
If you fail to plan, you're planning to fail.

All through my high school years, I was repeatedly told, "The key to your future is hidden in your daily routine." My mother planned her days and her weeks and, at times, was ridiculed by her own siblings for being too orderly and organized. Thank you, mom! Her gift of organization and planning has enabled me to stay ahead of the curve in my speaking profession and to build a business that is based on a strategic plan.

LESSON 30
Build a climate of confidence.

Information breeds confidence. Know what you believe and *why* you believe it. Disconnect the memory of past failures. Stop advertising your mistakes. Remind yourself of good decisions and triumphs in the past. See yourself succeeding. Deposit success pictures in the bank of your mind. Your mind is like a bank vault. It stores thousands of mental photographs of what you see, hear and think about most often. Mom always reminded me to think about God! My dominant thought patterns would reveal my true values. She was always reminding me to "fill up" in the morning with useful information that would shape my thoughts for the rest of the day. Your confidence will be shaped by taking in the *right* information on a daily basis. The more confident you become, the more successful you become. Confidence will not remove the obstacles or tough days, but rather allow you to look beyond them and succeed.

LESSON 31
Instead of taking prayer out of something, put it before everything.

If I left out this lesson, my King James version, front row Baptist mother would disown me. Actually, this has been the catalyst for my decision-making process. Whenever I have to make a decision, large or small, I have learned to take adequate time, to pray about it and to only make a decision after I have reflected on it. Too many times, as a Christian, I have been guilty of *"leaning on my own understanding"* and not practicing what I preach, or I should say, what my mother preaches.

LESSON 32
Leadership is taking people where they have never been.

If you're going to take someone where they have never been, it might be a good idea to go there first. Too many times we fall victim to the leadership theory of "the lost leading the lost." We expect people to follow us. Yet, when we are not sure of the direction, we frustrate ourselves and everyone else in the process. This lesson is directly correlated to Lesson 28. I have always said, "If you're not sure where you are heading, you will get where you are going—nowhere!"

Lesson 33
Things crumble with the erosion of values.

Since my early adulthood years, I have witnessed the decay of morals and values in this country. From television to radio, the classroom to the boardroom, our values have decayed to a point where nothing surprises me anymore. Company mission statements have become nothing more than fancy decorations strategically hung in visible places for people to see. Values will always reveal what you care about and what you stand for.

Lesson 34
Decide on your own worth and decide
how much happiness to expect.

Our self-image determines our focus, or what we allow ourselves to think about. A good self-image allows us to concentrate on compliments paid to us and the successes we have achieved. This is not to be confused with having a big head. Someone once remarked, "Conceit is a weird disease. It makes everyone sick except the one that has it!" Being egotistical and having a healthy self-love are complete opposites. My mother taught that EGO stood for Edging God Out. She said that God should be the center of my attention. People with huge egos need to be the center of attention, crave recognition and have little concern for those around them. When we genuinely appreciate our own worth, there is no need to tell the world how good we are. It is only the person who hasn't convinced himself of his own worth who proceeds to inform the rest of humanity of his worth.

LESSON 35
Forgive!

When we choose to forgive, a marvelous principle comes into operation. As we change, others change. As we alter our attitude toward others, they begin to alter their behavior. Somehow, the moment we choose to change the way we see things, others respond to our changed expectations. Of course, the hardest lesson I learned on forgiveness was to forgive myself. When we don't forgive ourselves, we are actually choosing to stay on a guilt trip so we can put ourselves through some extra mental anguish. My mother's advice on forgiveness was straight and to the point. She said, "When we blame God, others or ourselves, we are avoiding the real issue which is the need to do something about the problem." We always have a choice. We can get on with our lives and live in the now, or we can chain ourselves to grudges and upsets of the past.

LESSON 36
Life is not perfect.

On numerous occasions I have told an audience that I am an anal, compulsive, organized perfectionist. In Omaha, Nebraska, I was asked by a conference attendee the question we all have either been asked or, at the very least, have asked ourselves. "If you had your life to live over again, what would you do differently?" For those who know me, my response was not what you might expect. I said, "I wouldn't be so perfect!" Happiness is a decision and is based on making the most of what we've got. The degree of our unhappiness is the distance between the way things are and the way they "ought" to be. If we cease to demand that things be perfect, the business of being happy becomes easier. Just like my mother (a recovering perfectionist), when I learned to relax more, eat more ice cream and travel lighter, life became less stressful.

LESSON 37
Life is not that serious.

When you laugh, all kinds of wonderful things happen to benefit your body and mind. Endorphins are released in your brain giving you a natural "high" and giving your respiratory system the kind of workout that it might get from jogging. Laughter relieves pain. You can only laugh when you are relaxed and the more relaxed you are, the less pain you feel. Funny books and movies are ideal pain relievers. My wife and I have all the Seinfeld episodes on DVD. We are more relaxed and find ourselves in better moods when we watch an episode or twenty. In fact, you can't get ulcers and laugh at the same time—you choose to have one or the other. Periodically, let us remind ourselves that we are human and, as leaders, we do stupid things. If you expect to be perfect, you don't belong on the planet (note to self and my mother). Let's remember that our own troubles always seem bigger to us than to anyone else. If no one else is losing sleep, maybe we don't need to either.

LESSON 38
We attract what we fear.

Because the things that we most love and most fear tend to occupy our thoughts much of the time, we tend to attract those very things. Yet most people stagger through life bemoaning what they don't have and talking about what they don't want. It is a hopeless situation. We must focus on what we want. When we fear losing something, we place ourselves in a position to lose it. This applies to husbands, girlfriends, wallets, tennis matches and sports teams. We often find that once we decide to face the fear, it evaporates. No doubt you have had the experience of performing a task you thought would be difficult or particularly embarrassing. When you jumped in and did it, it wasn't half as bad as you anticipated. This particularly applies to telling the truth and owning up to mistakes and misdeeds. How often have you found that thinking about it was so much more painful than doing it?

LESSON 39
Put all you have into all you do.

Every parent, coach or teacher says the same thing, "All I ask is that you give me your best effort." I remember growing up having disillusions about this lesson. If you put all you have into whatever you do, you won't eliminate failure. If you put everything you have into everything you do, you won't eliminate disappointment. So, I would ask my mother, "Why bother?" Her answer was, "For your own self-respect." When your personal philosophy is "I will do my best, regardless," you will always stand tall in your own estimation. Losing hurts, but it hurts even more when you realize that you haven't done your best.

LESSON 40
Keep moving.

My father-in-law provides us with Lesson 40. Longevity statistics reveal that the average person doesn't last very long after retirement. My father-in-law, Bill Rohde, retired in May and died in November of the same year. The lesson here is "Don't retire, or don't retire too early!" If a fellow says, "I am 94 years old and I've worked all my life," we need to realize that may be how he got to be 94. George Bernard Shaw won a Nobel Prize when he was nearly 70. Benjamin Franklin produced some of his best writings at age 84, and Pablo Picasso put brush to canvas right through his eighties. Isn't the issue how old we think we are? We are what we think. I was always taught to surround myself with a character of people who resembled who I wanted to become. True! Now to add to that…surround yourself with people who resemble what you want out of life. A bonus is that while we keep moving, we don't have a chance to worry. Hence, we avoid the dreaded "paralysis by analysis." There is happiness and fulfillment in activity. This lesson encourages us to get off our back sides and to get involved.

LESSON 41
Use it or lose it.

Whatever we don't use, we lose. It is particularly easy to see this lesson at work in our physical bodies. If you decide to spend three years in a wheel chair for no other reason except that you like sitting down, when the three years are up, you won't be able to walk. Stop using your legs and they stop working. We have to keep using our mind to keep it in shape. There is no reason we should become less able as the years go by. If we keep using our mental capacity to the fullest, our mind will keep working for us.

LESSON 42
Life is worthless unless you give it value.

Life in itself has no value. Just because we are here does not mean that our lives have any value. Ultimately, only we decide whether our stay on this planet is to be our privilege and our joy, or whether it is to be a sentence of misery and despair. Life is not dull. There are many dull people who see their world through muddy, tainted glasses. Many people die at 25 but aren't buried until they are 70. It is a mystery to me how some people see beauty and magic everywhere they look, while others remain unmoved. No matter how much beauty and magic you have enjoyed up until now, you can choose to have more fun today. It is a choice, every day.

CONCLUSION

*Leadership is about living a life of lasting
impact and leaving a legacy of caring.*

Well, there you have it—*MUM'S THE WORD, a Mother's Lessons in Leadership*. Learn them and apply them to your life. If you lead by them, people will follow you.

As I put my thoughts on paper, it has been my prayer and my plan to share some information and inspiration that will make a difference in your life. The need for both information and inspiration in our personal and corporate worlds is enormous. The opportunity to benefit many people is great. My prayer is that some idea struck a responsive chord in you that will enable you to enjoy your life more and enable you to be even more effective as a leader.

So, as I end this book, it would only be appropriate to leave you with one last lesson my mother taught me.

"Every now and then—somewhere, some place, sometime—you are going to have to plant your feet, stand firm and make a point about who you are and what you believe in. When the time comes, Stephen, you simply have to do it." —Patricia L. Wise, 132 Brians Court, Portersville, PA 16051

RECOMMENDED READING

Carew, Don and Eunice Parisi-Carew, *High Five* (Morrow). The magic of working together

Collins, Jim, *Good to Great* (Harper Business). Why some companies make the leap…and others don't

De Bono, Edward, *Six Thinking Hats* (Back Bay Books). Your success will depend on how well you think

Drucker, Peter F., *Managing in a Time of Great Change* (Dutton). The guru of management shows us what is rather than what is supposed to be

Gilliland, Steve, *Enjoy The Ride* (Advantage). The true joy of life is in the trip. Keys to living a happy life and maintaining a positive outlook

Glaser, Judith E., *Creating We* (Platinum Press). How to build a healthy thriving organization; how to change "I" thinking to "we" thinking

Goleman, Daniel, *Working with Emotional Intelligence* (Bantam Books). A thoughtfully written, persuasive account explaining emotional intelligence and why it can be crucial to your career

Johnson, Spencer, M.D., *Who Moved My Cheese?* (Putnam). An amazing way to deal with change in your work and in your life

McGraw, Phillip C., PhD, *Self Matters* (Simon & Schuster). Creating your life from the inside out

Mackay, Harvey, *Swim with the Sharks* (Morrow). Out sell, out manage, out motivate and out negotiate your competition

Ziglar, Zig, *Top Performance* (Revell). How to develop excellence in yourself and others

PERSONAL
ACTION PLAN

Now that you have read this book, what impacted you most and will change the way you lead?

Specifically, how and what are you going to do, based on your answer to the first question?

To whom are you going to be accountable?

Additional resources developed by
Steve Gilliland are available from

Impact Store
877-499-8901

Through Impact Store, Steve Gilliland offers a wide range of books, CDs, videos and DVDs designed to increase an individual's ability to influence and lead others.

A unique resource is Steve's book, *Performance Essentials in the Work Place*. Imagine attending five insightful seminars on five of the hottest workplace topics and receiving five workbooks with the blanks already filled in. Add to that numerous inspirational thoughts and quotes from one of today's hottest speakers. Impact Store brings you a resource that will inspire, instruct and enable you to readily reference information on today's most important performance essentials: organization, attitude, customer service, teamwork and motivation. In addition, the book also includes over 100 of Steve Gilliland's signature quotes.

To receive a catalog of resources available from Steve Gilliland or information regarding his speaking itinerary, please call toll free 866-445-5452 or write:

Impact Store
2801 Freeport Road
Natrona Heights, PA 15065
www.impactstore.com

Steve Gilliland
P. O. Box 30220
Winston-Salem, NC 27130
www.stevegilliland.com